TINO TABAK

TINO TABAK

DREAMS AND DEMONS
OF A NEW ZEALAND CYCLING LEGEND

JONATHAN KENNETT

Copyright © 2009 Kennett Brothers Limited

First published by Kennett Brothers Limited 2009
Reprinted 2010

PO Box 11 310, Wellington, New Zealand
Phone/fax +64 4 499 6376
jonathan@kennett.co.nz
www.kennett.co.nz

Tino Tabak: Dreams and Demons of a New Zealand Cycling Legend is the fifth title in the *New Zealand Cycling Legends* series.

National Library of New Zealand Cataloguing-in-Publication Data
Kennett, Jonathan.
Tino Tabak: dreams and demons of a New Zealand cycling legend / Jonathan Kennett.
(New Zealand cycling legends)
Includes index.
ISBN 978-0-9582673-5-9
1. Tabak, Tino, 1946- 2. Cyclists—New Zealand—Biography. I. Title. II. Series.
796.62092—dc 22

All rights reserved. No part of this publication may be reproduced, stored in a retrieval system or transmitted, in any form or by any means without the prior written permission of the publisher, nor be otherwise circulated in any form of binding or cover other than that in which it is published and without a similar condition being imposed on the subsequent purchaser.

Every effort was made to ensure that the information in this book is accurate and to acknowledge sources and attain permissions for the images used. The author/publishers will be glad to rectify any mistakes or omissions at the earliest opportunity.

Cover design: Nick Turzynski
Front cover photographs: The Tabak Collection and the Neil Robinson Collection
Editing and production by Whitireia Publishing
This publication was produced by students on the publishing programme at Whitireia Polytechnic
www.whitireia.ac.nz
Printed and bound in New Zealand by Printlink

CONTENTS

Prologue	7
The New World	9
The Outsider	13
Firewind Champion	25
Learning to Ride	51
Breaking Away	69
A World Apart	77
The Sub-topper Years	95
Raleigh's Captain	105
Dreams and Demons	117
Finding Tino	133
Epilogue	137
Where Are They Now?	140
Key Race Results	141
New Zealanders in the Tour de France	146
Glossary	147
Sources	148
Out Takes	150
Acknowledgements	153
The Author	154
Index	155

Tino Tabak, 1972.   *The Tabak Collection*

PROLOGUE

This is my story. I'm only going to tell it once and then it's done. Not for a million dollars will I do this again.

Some people have already made up their minds about me. They say, 'Tino Tabak did this' or 'Tino Tabak did that'. If you're one of them, you might as well close this book right now, 'cause you've already closed your mind. Just put it back on the shelf and walk away. I've got no time for you.

But if you really want to know what the business of pro cycling was like in the seventies, I can tell you. Because I've been through it all – from being a star of the road at the top, to a pile of broken dreams at the bottom. Europe's greatest sport can do that to you.

Sometimes I wish I'd never left New Zealand.

TINO TABAK, 2009

THE NEW WORLD

Grey and weathered, the wooden gangway rose to the *Sibajak*, a reconditioned troop ship bound for New Zealand. On the wharf below, hundreds of tearful people sorted themselves into two groups – those who would stay and those who would go. Queues formed, papers were stamped, then a steady footfall sounded on the gangway planks. Some smiled with relief; others stared inwards with grief and trepidation.

Most of the Dutch emigrants that day were single men – young, healthy and desperate – beckoned by a growing country in need of hard workers. Among the few exceptions to climb the gangway were the Tabaks: father Gerben, mother Hendrika and six-year-old Tino. With each step, they climbed away from their home, their village, their whole way of life. They were leaving all that they loved about their country – and all that they loathed.

A dozen years earlier, as war clouds gathered over Europe, the Netherlands had chosen to stay neutral. It was a political balancing act that had served the nation well in the First World War but was untenable in the second. In May 1940, unprepared for German invasion, the land of dykes and windmills was defeated in only five days. Most of the Dutch army fought with pre-1900 weapons, a farcical match against Germany's military might. Over the following five years, the Netherlands was systematically ransacked. The Nazis took land, buildings, food and Jewish lives, all in vast quantities. Any resistance met with vicious reprisals, and civilians, including Gerben and Hendrika, were forced into terrible labour camps. Those who had argued that a peaceful occupation would be better than protracted war fell silent. When the Allies finally landed in Normandy on D-Day (6 June 1944), expectations were huge and triggered impromptu celebrations nationwide. But hopes were soon dashed, as liberation proved tortuously slow.

The Nazis' retreat from the Netherlands dragged on for nine months, and during the Hunger Winter of 1944–45 they left behind nothing they considered useful or edible. As the Allies battled their way north, the Dutch stuck behind enemy lines slowly starved, and resorted to eating tulip bulbs and sugar beets. Thousands died.

Gerben and Hendrika Tabak lived in the village of Enschede, near the north-eastern border with Germany. Among the last to be freed, they were traumatised by the horrors of the war.

An optimistic baby boom marked the resumption of peace and Jentinus (Tino) Johannes Tabak was born on 6 May 1946. Too late, the Dutch government realised that the challenges of a burgeoning population were being compounded by a slow economic recovery and high unemployment. Also, wartime divisions between collaborators and resisters inevitably led to years of bitterness and resentment as the Dutch blamed each other for their post-war predicament.

In a desperate move, the government and church authorities launched a huge campaign to convince people to leave their overcrowded homeland and seek a better life in the new world – most notably Canada, Australia and New Zealand. The Tabak family were among thousands that left in 1952; escaping the past in search of a better future, a future with hope and ambition. Yet for Hendrika and Tino, emigration was fraught with anxiety and apprehension. Gerben, on the other hand, showed no qualms or

Tino and his grandmother at Enschede, the Netherlands, in 1949. *The Tabak Collection*

Tino on board the *Sibajak*, en route to the new world in 1952. *The Tabak Collection*

fears. When the *Sibajak* slipped her moorings and steamed out of the harbour, the bold patriarch felt certain that the Netherlands was behind them for good. He had chosen New Zealand partly because he was following in brother Bert's footsteps, and partly because it was as far from Europe as he could get.

On the other side of the globe, a cautious and parochial New Zealand government sought as many suitable immigrants as possible to replace the men lost during the war. Applicants had to possess the right (that is, white) physical characteristics and mental attitude to be assimilated into the New Zealand way of life. Gerben Tabak appeared to fit the bill perfectly – he looked Anglo-Saxon and was eager to assume a new cultural identity.

When we finally reached New Zealand, I remember Dad saying proudly, 'I'm a Kiwi now.'

THE OUTSIDER

From the boat, Wellington was our first sight of New Zealand. It just looked so green and hilly – so different from home. Dad was grinning from ear to ear. It was a big adventure. Mum had tears running down her face. Even as a little kid you don't forget those things.

Early morning, December 1952; the *Sibajak* docked in Wellington harbour. Jaded travellers began to disperse, not randomly but by design. Pre-arranged jobs were scattered far and wide across the country. The conservative government – indeed most New Zealanders – wanted the 'aliens' to be assimilated as quickly as possible. By making it difficult to keep in contact with fellow immigrants, officials hoped the new arrivals would soon forget the culture of their past. Speaking Dutch in public, and in some cases even their own homes, was discouraged. Gerben Tabak may have declared, 'I am a Kiwi now,' but no matter how eager he was to fit in, he could never disguise the guttural accent that marked him as a foreigner.

From Wellington, the Tabak family took the night ferry to Lyttelton and were driven to their accommodation at Styx, north of Christchurch. Immediately Gerben started working for Tom Champion, a solid sheep farmer struggling to keep pace with an unprecedented wool boom. Before long, Gerben led his family to a more isolated farm tucked below Mt Thomas in North Canterbury.

New Zealand had been promoted as 'the land of the future', and Gerben only ever looked forward. On the farm, he quickly learnt from others, but he also developed his own skills. He showed Tino how to keep track of the time by making a sundial out of a round cowpat and a straight stick. And to supplement their dinner, father and son went eeling, using a hedgehog rolled in bailing twine as bait. Gerben also concentrated on learning English and the culture of the local community.

But at the farmhouse, with no electricity or sewerage, and no Dutch friends or village markets to provide a social lifeline, Tino's mother Hendrika looked backward, battling a terrible homesickness.

And Tino? Tino looked inward. Speaking no English, he was sent off to his first day at Papanui Primary School with a sign dangling from his neck that read, 'Tino Tabak – Dutch Boy.' Kids crowded around the playground novelty, pressing in, jostling and staring. They marvelled at his bleach-blond hair and brilliant blue eyes. Just as some shout at the deaf, they raised their voices to be understood: 'Hello Dutch boy; hello Dutch boy …' Blind to the smiles of possible friendship, Tino turned and fled, running for all he was worth from the strangeness of this new land.

Throughout his childhood, as the family moved through various farms around Canterbury, Tino found security in his own company, inventing his own games and making his own rules. His interest in sport was already strong. Listening avidly to rugby and soccer on the radio, he would race around the yard, replaying the moves of both sides, and the referee. Gerben also listened to sport, and despite his resolve to become a Kiwi, he could not resist the lure of tuning into Dutch radio to follow the great Tour de France. From 1953 to 1961 it was contested by national teams, and even thousands of miles away it drew passionate interest from almost all European immigrants.

Tino and his mother, Hendrika Tabak. *The Tabak Collection*

When Tino was ten years old, Corrie was born. Tino's younger brother suffered from rheumatic fever and so the family ended their nomadic lifestyle and settled in Hornby, on the outskirts of Christchurch, close to doctors. While attention turned to nursing Corrie to health, Tino was largely left to himself and continued to develop into a strong, self-reliant loner with little respect for authority.

By contrast, Gerben became more and more involved with the

local community, joining the Hornby Working Men's Club and the local branch of the Labour Party. Years later he became known by children as the Father Christmas at Hornby Mall, and by adults as the president of Hornby Cycling Club. Eventually, in 1990, the mayor of Christchurch, Vicki Buck, would present him with the New Zealand Commemoration Medal in recognition of his services to the community.

Although Gerben threw himself into the New Zealand way of life, he had his limits. With the atrocities of war etched on his mind, he could not restrain outrage when Tino came home from school one day in cadet uniform. The Dutchman had a horror of military regimes and could not accept New Zealand's pro-military culture. He forbade his son's involvement in cadet training. Once again, Tino was marked as 'different'.

Like most old-world immigrants, Gerben's sporting interests centred on the Olympics, cycling and soccer. He had been a top soccer player in the Netherlands and once the family was settled in Hornby, Gerben organised the building of a soccer field, which has since evolved into Waiola Park. He also formed the Neelandia soccer team and arranged a multitude of club matches. Tino discovered his own talent for soccer, which greatly boosted his morale – but his loner temperament was more suited to cycling.

In soccer I had to work with a team, but in cycling I could do what I wanted, when I wanted.

Dutch immigrants talked with fervour of the famous European races and riders, and Tino soon became fired with a passion for cycle racing. As young as ten years old, he dreamed of riding the Tour de France. Often on the way to and from his new school in Hornby, schoolmates, some on proper racing bikes, would challenge him: 'Betcha I can beat you.' Straining on the pedals of his old black bitser, he soon left them for dead.

Tino poses for
The Evening Post
on a novel fold-
away bicycle.
*Alexander Turnbull
Library, Evening Post
Collection, ref no.
EP/1967/5649*

At the age of 12 or 13, Tino entered a road race organised by the local cash club, the Hornby Wheelmen. As a novice, the unknown boy was given a good handicap and sent off 15 minutes ahead of the top riders. This egalitarian characteristic of the New Zealand racing system gave everyone an equal chance of winning, but it made no sense to Tino.

I remember arguing with the official when they gave me my trophy, 'How could I win, when you sent me off first? I wasn't the best.'

From that day on I was totally against handicap racing. All I wanted was to start from the back mark, with the scratch riders, because they are the best. They're the real winners. Then years later I even wanted to start behind scratch, and sometimes I did. In the Christchurch to Akaroa one year, I was lined up there with the scratch riders, and when they said, 'Go', I just sat back on my bike and waited. I got a few odd looks of course. After a minute, I took off and still won the race.

By the age of 14 Tino was struggling academically. Lacking from the Riccarton High School syllabus was his favourite subject – cycling. Instead, he was top of the class at scrubbing desks (during detentions) and an expert at anticipating the strike of whistling bamboo upon his backside. So Tino would skip classes to train, and as soon as he turned 15, he left school for good. With no qualifications, he drifted into the railways as an apprentice boilermaker at the Addington Railway Workshops. It was the perfect place for an aspiring cyclist: the work wasn't demanding and the hours were flexible enough to allow trips away for races.

Gerben Tabak committed himself as enthusiastically to his son's passion for cycling as he did to any of his community projects. He provided advice, mechanical support, transport to races and, of course, Tino's first racing bike, a second-hand Holdsworth from the local bike shop. It had a grey steel frame, ten gears and aluminium water bottles mounted on the handlebars. Competitive cycling was a growing sport among Kiwi amateurs. The road season ran from early winter to Christmas. Everyone then switched to track racing for a few months. Young boys such as Tino started in the novice grade and, after a couple of seasons, pedalled their way through the junior ranks, hoping after a few years to challenge the only other grade left — the seniors. There were no veteran or masters grades in those days, because Kiwi blokes usually gave up competitive cycling once they got married. Older men often helped to run the sport, as Gerben did for many years. At the ages of 16 and 17, Tino competed in 82 races and won 47 fastest times. Gerben was the proudest father in Christchurch.

Tino's hero of the time was Jacques Anquetil — holder of the world hour record and five-time winner of the Tour de France. Tino knew that the French rider's father had been a farmer — like Gerben — and that Anquetil admired hard physical work. Uncompromising and disliked by many, Anquetil typically raced from the front, alone. It wasn't difficult for Tino to model himself on the European champion — they had much in common. He soon had a cycling jersey knitted that was the same as Anquetil's, and he emulated his hero's racing and training techniques.

I had this kind of weird film in my mind of European races. The Gorges [in Canterbury] was Paris–Roubaix. Christchurch to Akaroa was a mountain stage in the Tour de France. Even training was a race — it was a dream … a fantasy. Sometimes I was Anquetil the champion, powering ahead of the peloton, sweeping around the bends and through the crowds. The bunch chased and chased, but Tino-Anquetil just rode harder … all the way to the finishing line — then home: real life again.

Tino developed his own strict training schedule that included rides on Sunday, Monday, Tuesday, Wednesday and Thursday.

Didn't matter if it was rain, hail or snow — I'd do the rides I'd planned. Occasionally the other boys would ask to train with me. I'd tell them when and where to meet, but I'd never wait for them, or stop to regroup at the top of a hill, or at a milkbar as they used to. No way! And they weren't allowed to ride beside me. I'd half-wheel them [ride half a wheel in front] until they dropped in behind, then just try to get rid of them. To put it plainly, I'd thrash hell out of them.

On Friday I'd rest and pull the whole bike to bits on the kitchen table. Everything would be cleaned and oiled. Ball bearings, the lot. Then I'd be in bed by 8:30pm and listen to the Stan Williams sports programme on the radio before going to sleep. It was always the other boys that got mentioned, never me. At times I couldn't sleep I was so wild. I thought, 'Why don't they mention me?'

Saturday was the real race day, but it didn't always live up to the dream. Some of the Canterbury juniors were very fast, and they certainly knew how to sprint. For Tino, John Cleary provided an infuriating challenge. An unassuming-looking boy with thick glasses that belied an impressive skill at bike racing, he had a sprint that often got the better of Tino.

John Cleary was always a pain in the butt. I came up through the ranks with him, but he was a better sprinter. I had to do something to beat him. So I tried sitting on his wheel and sprinting him, but then they disqualified me for not taking a turn at the front. Said it wasn't sportsmanlike. What a load of rubbish! In Europe the first man across the line was the winner, no matter how they got there. End of story!

Tino hated being beaten by Cleary, and after such races refused to speak to him. But irksome as he found Cleary, it wasn't really personal. Tino was simply committed to beating any rider who lined up beside him. The best Cantabrian riders were in the Papanui club and went to Laurie Dawe Cycles. So Tino joined the Mairehau Novice Cycling Club and favoured a small bike shop in Hornby. He didn't want anything to do with the other racers except beat them.

Canterbury's top juniors – from left, Graeme Sword, Tino Tabak, John Cleary and Mike Litolff – poised to win the national 4,000-metre team pursuit title in 1963. *Wayne Thorp Collection*

John Cleary, Wayne Thorpe and Laurie Dawe were a cliquey group that I rebelled against. But it was very healthy competition.

After the race-day prize-giving, Tino would head home and clean up before rushing back into town to buy the sports paper to see if he was mentioned. Then it was party time. Every Saturday he would party up, drink lots and forget about cycling. For many, this was the public face of Tino Tabak, and he soon gained a reputation as a wild young drunkard. But the public perception often obscured the serious intent that powered Tabak's obsession:

Sunday morning, I was up at 8am, and by 9am I was on the bike, training.

In May 1965, Tino turned 19. He was restless. Even his accommodating employer presented an impediment to his cycling mania. He felt the surge of his potential and wanted the chance to pit himself against the challenges offered in senior cycling. As a junior he had placed sixth against the seniors in both the Timaru to Christchurch and the Tour of Southland. It was time to step up. With six months of his apprenticeship to go, he quit the railways and started cycling fulltime, occasionally taking on contract work in forestry around Canterbury and at the freezing works in Invercargill to pay the bills. Tino was entering a new phase of cycling – the fulltime amateur.

Tino on his second racing bike, a Carlton, circa 1964.   *The Tabak Collection*

FIREWIND CHAMPION

I just wanted to be the best. With the best, in the best, better than the best. It sounds very arrogant, I know, but that was me at the time.

In 1965, the New Zealand cycling landscape was tilted on its axis, toppling the established contenders and leaving the whole field gasping to keep up. This was the beginning of a three-year period that proved ground-breaking for Tino – as well as for New Zealand cycling. The young rider's colourful personality, rebellious nature and movie star looks revitalised the sport. He infuriated uncompromising racing officials, demoralised champions and flirted with a fan club of dizzy teenage girls. Tabak was the first modern celebrity of New Zealand cycling, and the media soon learned that simply by following him they were guaranteed a story.

Veteran cycling journalist Alan Messenger recalls that Tino was always featured on television's *Grandstand*. 'Cycling got more publicity than it ever had, before or since, and it was all because of Tabak.' Throughout the notoriety and fame, however, Tino remained committed to his single, long-standing ambition – to ride the Tour de France.

As always, the road season started in early winter, with short

Tino Tabak, left, and Bill Kendell fly through a small town on the Round the Gorges Classic.
The Tabak Collection

provincial races up to two hours long. By now Tabak was riding so brilliantly that, even though he was still a junior, the handicappers placed him on scratch with the best senior riders. In October he entered three major South Island classics. He won fastest time in the first two and in the third, the Timaru to Christchurch, he was nudged into second fastest time by former national road champion Tony Ineson. The tall Southlander could sprint, climbed like a goat and had years of experience to call upon. What Ineson the veteran understood, and Tabak the rookie had yet to overcome, was the critical role that air resistance played in cycling.

Air resistance – the faster a bunch rides, the more it dominates. At speeds over 30 kilometres per hour, riders sheltering in the bunch have a 30 per cent advantage. Every rider wants that advantage, to rest in preparation and be ready for the final sprint, yet every bunch must have its front riders. With this dilemma the tension that pervades competitive cycling begins: the workers versus the wheel suckers, the endurance athletes versus the sprinters. Only in time trials, 'the race of truth' in which riders are sent off at one-minute intervals, is there no place to shelter. There the group tension dissolves.

Like his hero Jacques Anquetil, Tabak lacked an explosive finishing burst. In a mad mass dash to the finish, such riders always struggle to win – usually being blown away by sprinters who have often 'wheel-sucked' their way to the finish. Lacking pure speed, Tabak soon realised he couldn't afford to stay with the bunch until the final charge. He had no choice but to ignore the alluring shelter and attempt to break away on his own – forcing the pace, forcing it again and again, until he had ripped the legs off every good rider in the peloton, especially the sprinters.

In handicap races such as Canterbury's 100-mile Round the Gorges Classic, there were usually only a few scratch riders to worry about. Those sent off in the earlier starts merely needed to be reeled in, not out-sprinted on the line, and that presented no problem for an exceptional time-trialler such as Tabak. Large parts of the Gorges course were gravel, which made drafting difficult, and there were hills he could break away on. And so, in 1965, Tino snared fastest time in the Round the Gorges in just over four hours. His time was 13 minutes faster than Warwick Dalton's 1959 course record.

The following weekend Tabak made his way to Invercargill, where he lined up against a more complete field for the 522-kilometre Tour of Southland. They didn't know what hit them. Tabak tyrannised the time trial, was first-equal in the King of the Mountains, and won the overall tour by three minutes. Forty-three tours later, and he still stands as the youngest rider to have won the Tour of Southland. The time trial was pivotal – from this point on Tabak won every time trial he entered in New Zealand. It was his trump card, and he used it to great effect.

The 1965 road season ended on 4 December with the 100-mile National Road Championships in Dunedin. This was Tino's biggest test to date, and in an attempt to qualify for the 1966 Commonwealth Games he had chosen to enter the senior race, rather than take his place in the junior event. All the riders, including the best sprinters, would line up together and by now everyone knew the 19-year-old Tabak was a threat. Top contenders from as far as Auckland had assembled and some of the older riders almost succeeded in psyching out the young Tabak. Friend and cycling veteran Alan Messenger had driven a nervous Tino down to Dunedin and was staying at the same hotel. He remembers finding the younger rider in the bar the night before the race, unable to sleep and agonising over whether to switch to the junior championships. Alan reassured him by explaining, 'If you don't win tomorrow, they'll say it was understandable because you were a junior. But, if you do win … then what will they say?'

'Tabak was told pre-race that he had little show against the "Guns" but his answer to that comment was to attack all day and kick away in the last two kilometres,' reported Clayton Yaxley.

The national championships epitomised Tabak's developing style: to ride from the front so aggressively that he wore his rivals down before the final dash to the line. Critics claimed it was his only tactic, that he lacked cunning and didn't race strategically. Without a killer sprint, however, what options did he have? Although it seemed crazy to attack repeatedly, that's what Tabak had to do to avoid a sprint finish. When he made his final serious breakaway, on the cusp of a sharp hill two kilometres from the finish, his opponents seemed unable to respond. 'TABAK FIRST – DAYLIGHT SECOND' exclaimed one newspaper headline. Behind 'daylight' was a peloton led by former champion Tony Ineson.

I told myself I was going to win the New Zealand road champs in Dunedin when I was 19 years old. People didn't think I could do it. They thought I was arrogant. But people don't know me, and they don't know what I'm thinking. I had a plan to break away on the hill on the last round – so said, so done. And I won it.

Over the following year, Tabak wore the New Zealand championship jersey at every opportunity. He was voted 1966 Canterbury Sportsman of the Year as well as 1966 Cyclist of the Year. Flush with success and confidence, he focused on the Commonwealth Games in Jamaica. He trained hard for the selection trials and was duly placed in the games team, along with veteran riders such as Laurie Byers and the Thompson brothers, Des and Richie. After months of preparation, Tabak's first experience of overseas competition was a debacle. The race started at 6:35am on a slightly dewy road. Hurtling down the first hill, one of the leaders slid out of control, triggering a spectacular pile-up that halted all but six riders. After the crash the Kiwi team was split. Tino and Richie (with a buckled wheel) chased hard over many miles but never caught the front bunch. Laurie Byers and Des Thompson fought their way to the front and finished

Tabak attacks his seniors on the last hill in the 1965 National Road Championships, contested over 100 miles. In his wake, from left to right, are Dave Grave, Neil Robinson, Tony Ineson and Brian Manning.   *Neil Robinson Collection*

second and third respectively. Tabak, trailing in at 15th, was shattered. After the race he went out on the town with another young rider, got drunk and was picked up by police for indecent exposure at a nightclub. The New Zealand Amateur Cycling Association was furious. It called the renegade to appear before the council and account for his actions; when he refused, it suspended him from all licensed racing for three months. The young rebel shrugged his shoulders and focused on his European racing dreams.

With the Tour de France his motivation for every turn of the pedal, Tabak looked to the classic New Zealand stage races – the Tour of Southland, the Tour of Manawatu and the Dulux Six Day Cycle Race.

In 1966, he travelled to the North Island, where he claimed victory in the Manawatu and Dulux tours, before returning south to sweep the pool with his second Southland win. In the 20-year period that all three tours were run, no other cyclist managed such a feat.

According to former road champion Alf Ganderton, 'Tabak's determination and aggression was always a tad above all the best riders. He never gave in or showed he was tired in a race. His power of recovery between stages in the Dulux was quite exceptional.'

Tabak's tactics for the 1967 Dulux tour were executed to perfection. He started the tour in high spirits, having just won the Tour of Manawatu and been pumped up with the very latest preparation for athletes, a vitamin B12 injection. This popular placebo made riders think, 'I'm on B12 – I'll fly.' In the first four days Tabak rode well, but not *too* well. He knew he was a marked man and wanted to bide his time. Meanwhile, the brilliant kilo champion Harry Kent and the veteran Tony Ineson shone out as star riders.

The second to last stage was a 34-kilometre time trial between

Tino Tabak wins the 1965 National Road Championships.
The Dominion Post Collection

TOUR DE FRANCE DOWN UNDER

In the sixties the Dulux was the ultimate race that every rider aspired to ride and do well in. It was the greatest challenge of the cycling season. – Dulux contender Kevin Manning

The Dulux Six Day Cycle Race, successor to the Wisemans Tours of the 1950s, began in 1960 and ran for 25 years. Inspired by European tours, the Dulux was a world-class event, covering a wide range of terrain and passing through as many towns as possible between Auckland and Wellington. It's easy to see why the Dulux was Tabak's favourite event.

Racers covered an unprecedented 1,000 kilometres in one week. In 1966, possibly assisted by a persistent nor'wester, they averaged 38.5 kilometres per hour (almost 2kmh faster than that year's Tour de France winner). Race organisers offered sprint prizes along each stage and handed out thousands of small flags to school children on the route.

Prize trophies for the top 20 general classification riders and top ten King of the Mountain riders were added to the sprint trophies. Because this was an amateur event, prizes were called 'trophies' and had to be engraveable. There were more than 200 per tour, and they included anything from stereograms to salad servers. In 1967, Tino won a fine set of silver cutlery – one of the few possessions he was to take to Europe.

The Dulux Six Day Cycle Race was the pinnacle of New Zealand road racing, and a testing ground for anyone intending to graduate to Europe. Drawn-out battles between the great riders were broadcast throughout New Zealand, helping to make them household names.

When new management at Dulux withdrew their sponsorship, the quietly spoken, 71-year-old organiser, Alvyn Pennington, retired. Over the 25 years Pennington ran the event, he never paid himself a cent. For his efforts, he was made an MBE, which he considered priceless.

Wearing the yellow jersey, Tino leads the peloton uphill in the 1966 Dulux tour. Gary Vincent Collection

Palmerston North and Shannon. For two months, Tabak had trained on this stretch of the course, and he knew every inch of the road. He powered from one minute behind the yellow jersey to leading by 2 minutes 18 seconds. As soon as the 21-year-old Tino had taken the leader's yellow jersey, his mother and brother rushed to catch the ferry to Wellington, hoping to celebrate with him after the final stage. They would not be disappointed.

The competition was so demoralised that on the final day's ride into Wellington, Tabak broke away and gained almost two more minutes on his closest rivals. 'Oh son, you were great!' exclaimed Hendrika Tabak.

Celebrating his second victory in the Dulux tour in 1967, with his brother, Corrie, and mother, Hendrika. *Alexander Turnbull Library, Evening Post Collection, EP/1967/5171*

Two weeks later Tabak won the Tour of Southland by over four minutes. For the second year in a row he had won all three tours. Then – in Anquetil-esque fashion – he broke the national hour record. What else could he do in New Zealand? And what could the competition do to stop him?

In an article entitled 'Tremendous Tino's Second Grand Slam', Pete Smith wrote: 'The trouble now is that most of Tabak's principal rivals – and the class of the top dozen probably is higher than at any stage in the sport's history – seem content to race for second place whenever they meet up with the tenacious Tino.

'On the last stage of the recent six-day race … Tabak jumped away coming down into Wellington. Several of the following bunch had the strength and the speed to bridge the gap up to him, but all apparently felt that by doing so they might tow another rival up with them and the man who had got that "easy" ride could then turn around and take the sprint.

'I don't quite know how to overcome this sort of thinking but I do know that it is doing neither the sport nor the riders much good.'

Like many young men, Tabak couldn't stand to be ordered around. He was contemptuous of narrow-minded officials who demanded conformity from 'their' riders.

I did it my way whether they liked me or not. But in the end they had to select me because I was the best. My way of training worked for me. I hated people telling me I had to do anything – 'Hang on. The only thing I have to do is breathe!'

Eager to follow the great European riders, Tabak was determined to work his way through the amateur ranks before turning pro. This didn't stop him from defying convention and ultimately helping to evolve the amateur code for cycling in New Zealand. 'Tino Tabak did the right things at the wrong time,' reflected Keith Brown, a professional road champion of the time. An incident at the 1966 Timaru to Christchurch was a case in point. The race rules stipulated that every rider must race with a bell, although officials seldom insisted on it. Tino knew that in Europe, racing bikes never had bells on them, so his mind was made up.

There was definitely no room on my bike for a bell. End of story!

Not quite. On this particular day, the official checking all the bikes before the race was Stan Williams, a sports commentator who mentioned Tabak only when he had to. The malcontent was fined five shillings, to be paid before the race. Tabak declared he would pay the fine *after* the race, not before. That wasn't good enough for race referee Harry Litolff, and in the ensuing stand-off Gerben Tabak protested his son's case. The officials would not relent. Not for Tino or his foreign father.

Indignant, father and son returned to their car and prepared to head home. Suddenly, Tino declared, 'That's all right, Dad. I'll fix them.' As the scratch bunch disappeared up the road Tino prepared to cycle after them on his way home.

Reporter Clayton Yaxley summed up the maverick: 'Treating the day as an unscheduled training ride, Tabak chased the scratch bunch, caught them and cruised past with absolute contempt. Taking nothing away from the Fastest Time recipient Dave Grave, it was totally obvious that had Tabak started it would have been his victory.'

Tabak sliced his way through the whole field. He ended the ride with a cavalcade of cars following him in to Christchurch, thinking he was the winning rider. Anticipating trouble, Tabak pulled off the course just before the finish. None the less, the chief referee suspended him for 'an undisclosed reason'.

However, no one could find a rule that forbade a cyclist from riding through the field of a major race, so the suspension was soon dropped. But the rule to have a bell on racing bikes remained for another ten years.

The bell incident proved minor compared with the way Tabak flouted other elements of the amateur code. According to his racing licence, he was never to race for money. But cycling was expensive. As his prizes began to pile up – at one stage he possessed 20 canteens of cutlery – the solution seemed obvious, and once again Gerben stepped forward to help. For years, Gerben – a long-time lover of garage sales – had been buying boxes of assorted junk at city auctions to sell at weekends. Now, he began adding Tino's prizes to the garage sales; then, encouraged by success, he started touting for business at the bike races, virtually selling Tino's prize booty behind the podium.

Tino also accepted sponsorship from the Black Tulip, a Dutch-owned cafe at Motukarara, en route to Akaroa. He wore a distinctive Black Tulip uniform, and the cafe proprietors paid his travel expenses. It was a fine line, but a popular one. Within a year, five riders were riding under the Black Tulip banner, forming a team in what was – at least publicly – an individual sport. Private alliances had existed in New Zealand cycling for decades, but the Black Tulip was the first amateur team to display its business sponsorship publicly.

Tabak had no strong desire to race in a team but he enjoyed exploring the potential of team tactics ... and the stir they could cause. He was usually too far out the front, however, to gain much benefit from teammates.

As Tabak continued to polarise, he garnered a growing number of rivals and supporters. 'Every time that Tabak fastens his toe-straps in top company he is the target of everyone's attentions,' one reporter observed. In the 1966 National Road Championships

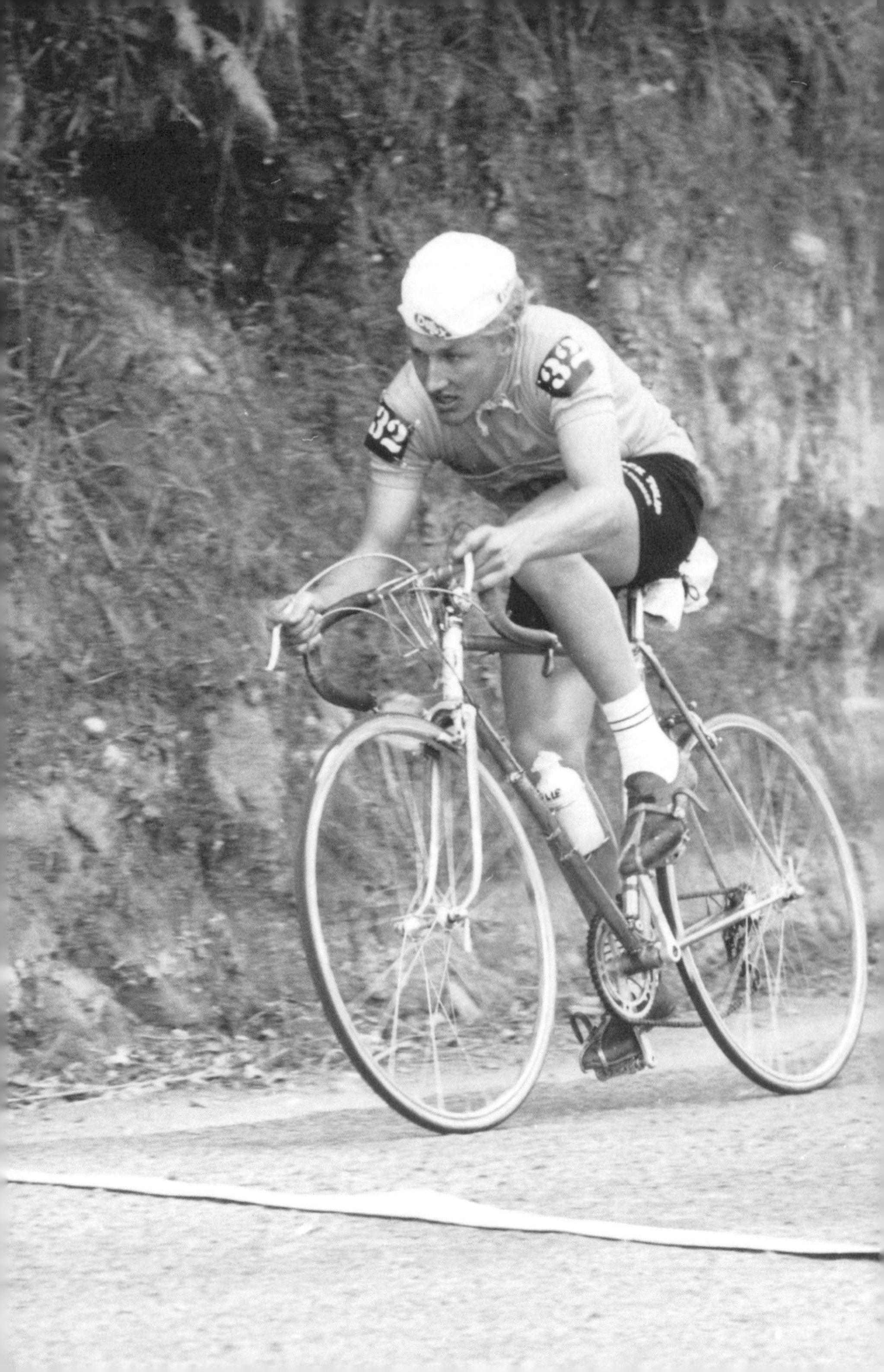
32
32

Tabak wins the grade-1 Mt Messenger hill climb from Gary King, Roy Jenkins (Australia) and Mal Powell (Australia) on the 188-kilometre Otorohanga to New Plymouth stage in the 1966 Dulux tour. These four rode brilliantly to beat the main bunch in to New Plymouth by a staggering seven and a half minutes.
Alexander Turnbull Library, Evening Post Collection, PAColl-1402-4-001

outside Napier, the top contenders were so busy covering Tabak's repeated attacks that they let an unfavoured Southlander, Graham Hill, nip away over the last hill. The chasing bunch of eight riders either didn't have the strength to hook on or, more likely, expected Tabak to pull the break back, so Hill went on to win by 80 seconds. In the sprint for the minor medals Tabak finished strongly behind Neil Robinson to take the bronze medal.

When well-known riding friend Ross Bush was asked why some people didn't like Tabak his response was emphatic: 'Jealousy – absolute jealousy! He was so damn good, that's why people didn't get on with him. There might have been a little of that Dutch arrogance as well.'

However, there was also considerable support for Tabak. Though most of it came from superficial fans enamoured with his looks and charisma, some of it was genuinely helpful. Whenever he was suspended, an eager reporter or a local official would argue his case. When Tabak suffered mechanical problems during a race his clubmates Roger Fowler and Ross Bush did not hesitate to sacrifice their own wheels, or even a whole bike. His father Gerben gave him advice and drove Tino to races all around the South Island. And when he was racing in the North Island, the Vertongens of Palmerston North made him feel part of the family.

Max Vertongen, a talented rider just a little younger than Tabak, recalls the South Islander being a gentleman who always helped around the house. Out on the road it was a different story: Vertongen never saw anyone train more aggressively than Tino Tabak. 'It was always flat out, 100 per cent. Most of the locals couldn't stay with him. He was time trialling – constantly looking at his watch.'

RACING IN AUSTRALIA

In August 1967, Tabak won the Air New Zealand Cycling Grand Prix two-day stage race at Palmerston North. This earned him selection for the tough Examiner Tour of the North in Tasmania, accompanied by a flock of flying Kiwis: Alf Baker, Bryce Beeston, Jack Broome, Derek Brown and Merv Davis. Tino was fit and confident. By the end of stage three, which he won by a country mile, he was so far in front the Australian press were comparing him to Hubert Opperman, the outstanding Aussie cyclist of the 1920s and 1930s. But they also noted: 'Tabak is obviously one of those characters who attract trouble without having to go and look for it.'

The race referee, Rex Blazely, might have been a sergeant major in a previous life, and the audacious Tabak was soon targeted. Over the 800-kilometre, 11-stage tour, conflict sparked, ignited – and blazed.

An article at the time, 'Tabak Victimised', described the conflict: 'The first brush between the two came after about 20 miles when Tabak opened up a half-mile gap on the rest of the field and [Blazely] insisted on controlling the race from a car barely ten yards in front of Tabak while the main bunch was out of sight down the road.'

I yelled at him to get out of the way … I couldn't see where I was going and the car tyres were throwing up water at me.

After the second stage, Blazely fined Tabak two dollars for removing a hand from the handlebars because he felt it was dangerous to do so in the middle of 40 riders on a wet road. He also fined him for sitting up and looking round when in the lead. Tabak retorted:

I don't have eyes in the back of my head and can't see how far in front I am unless I turn around. As for the hand removing, everyone changes their grip on a long ride, and in any case, I had to wipe the torrential rain from my eyes.

44 TINO TABAK: DREAMS AND DEMONS

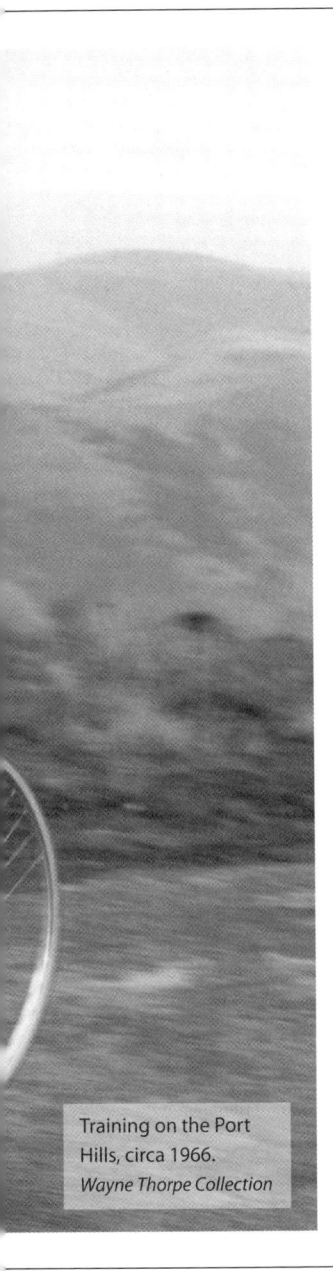

THE BAYS

Brakes, wheels, saddle ... a last check after breakfast before he's zipping down the drive, heading south on his favourite training ride.

Breakfast's well digested by the time he reaches Taitapu. 15 km: the first spot to take a time check: 29 minutes.

The now deserted road skirts snugly around the abrupt Banks Peninsula hills, to Motukarara and the Black Tulip. 25 km: 46 minutes.

Heading north-east now. The hills close in and the gravel begins just as the road tilts upwards to Gebbies Pass (155 metres high). Four kilometres of steep climbing. 29 km: 58 minutes.

Stay sharp for the screaming descent to the harbour. At the bottom, a few flat kilometres before the road twists and bucks around the bays to Lyttelton. 47 km: 1 hour 34 minutes.

The final climb, and it's a beauty – Evans Pass (200 metres). Tino digs in and powers to the top. A glance at the views, before sweeping down to Sumner. 55 km: 1 hour 52 minutes.

Now it's 'piano piano' – soft-pedalling the last 20 kilometres back to Hornby after three hours in the saddle. Another ride over. Another step towards his goal.

I loved riding the Bays. It was a little bit like I am – a change of character all the way. Uphill, downhill, a bit of flat, some false flats. Every time you went round a corner there was something different.

Training on the Port Hills, circa 1966.
Wayne Thorpe Collection

That night, Blazely assembled the entire New Zealand team and gave them an hour-long tongue-lashing. Later, Tabak drew Blazely's ire once more for pushing teammate Derek Brown up a hill. This time Mr Cardwell, the Auckland Cycling Centre president, spoke out: 'It is common practice for cyclists around the world to help their teammates along with a push in races of this type.'

A spirit of teamwork was beginning to kindle among the New Zealand riders, including Tabak. *The Examiner* newspaper reported: 'On stage 7 Tabak offered tour leader Derek Brown one of his wheels when he lost a swag of spokes in a collision. The ref wasn't having any of this and so Brown continued with his bike sounding like a xylophone as the loose spokes hit the forks.'

Later in the same stage the Australian champion Peter McDermott was involved in a serious crash. He'd been run off the road, and crossed the finish line covered in blood. The Australian officials wanted retribution and as Tabak was so clearly the villain of the tour they demanded his disqualification. Blazely was quick to oblige even though Tabak had had nothing to do with the crash. For a minute it looked as if the New Zealand team were ready to respond by pulling out, but manager Rob Sowry was smarter than that. He waited until the riders were lining up for the next stage and then appealed against the decision. The tour was running late and all the arrival times had been advertised, so there was no time to hear the appeal. Blazely was forced to let Tabak race under appeal.

One magazine later reported: 'The disqualification hearing itself had been real entertainment. Tabak was jumping up and down like a yo-yo and waving his arms around in all directions: Mr Blazely was equally as excited; press and television cameras recorded it all for posterity; other officials shooed away hundreds of kids.'

The disqualification was ultimately lifted and replaced with a five-minute time penalty, putting Tabak out of contention for the tour. But Blazely wouldn't accept any half measures. The following day he resigned from his post with the Tasmania Amateur Cyclists Union. The race rules clearly forbade 'collusion' (that is, teamwork), and after the tour Tabak surprised one reporter, Cecil Cripps, by revealing:

The referee was right in disqualifying me. He is the first referee I've struck who has had the courage to tell you exactly what he thinks of you, and that's the type of man I like. He did a really good job!

On the fourth and final day, the Examiner Tour was won by Tabak's teammate Alf Baker. Tabak was quoted by NZPA: 'The whole idea of the Air New Zealand trip was that we get one of our team to win this race. It's a New Zealand victory that counts – nothing else.'

Tabak had held back with the bunch in the last stage, keeping them alive with his 'good natured banter and antics', at one stage throwing small firecrackers among the riders. He finished eighth, his worst tour result to date, but was heralded as the hero of the team. This was probably the only time that the majority of the New Zealand cycling community bonded with Tino.

Shortly after, Tabak received a phone call from Australian promoter Bill Long, offering him a professional deal. 'I would pay Tabak to race tomorrow,' said Long, who was looking for a charismatic Kiwi to fill the cycling shoes of Warwick Dalton (the Kiwi legend who raced as an Australian pro from 1962 to 1966). 'He is just the type of rider the crowds would love.' Impressed as the Australian was with the young New Zealander, the feeling was not reciprocated and Australia played no further part in Tabak's cycling ambitions.

Acts of team camaraderie may run counter to Tabak's reputation as a self-centred loner, but they reflect the complexity of his personality. Having proved he was the best, Tino occasionally stepped back from the role of aggressive challenger. He did just that in the Shirley Lodge Classic, a tough 80-miler around North Canterbury.

Starting as a scratch marker in that race, Tino ripped through the field until he reached the lone front marker — old George McGregor. Poor George was only a mile from the finish when he heard a cyclist fast approaching from behind. Looking over his shoulder, he exclaimed, 'Oh shit! That's not you is it, Tino?' 'It is, George,' Tabak replied. Line honours would have meant a lot to most riders, but on that day, not to Tino.

'Tabak made one of the finest gestures I have ever seen in my time of watching and reporting sport of all kinds,' wrote veteran reporter Ray Cairns. 'He encouraged McGregor to keep going, then pushed him ahead at the finish line, telling him to raise his hand in a victory salute.'

Tabak broke the Australasian hour record, at English Park, in 1966 and again in 1967. *The Tabak Collection*

It was generosity that Tabak rarely had a chance to show, and it formed one of his happiest memories of racing in New Zealand. It also broke Rule 101: 'Competitors shall ride to win.'

That was one rule Tino was 100 per cent behind, most of the time. And at 21, he was ready to broaden his winning horizons. As reporter Pete Smith observed in an article of late 1967, he had outgrown local racing:

'What does the future hold for Tabak? At 21, he's gone about as far as he can go here, unless he should be content to stay on, train away and clean up all the stage races, season after season, until someone better comes along, and who knows how long that might be?'

Content? Tabak was certainly not content. Success in New Zealand simply fuelled his dream to ride the Tour de France.

After setting the hour record [December 7, at English Park, Christchurch] I decided, 'That's it. Time to go.' I bought a one-way ticket for the day after tomorrow. Packed a few things – not much. I had a hundred pounds, my summer clothes and the silver cutlery set I'd won in the Dulux. My mum was at the boat to see me off, no one else. I was finally on my way to learn how to ride a bike.

LEARNING TO RIDE

Amsterdam. Christmas 1967. Throughout the festive season, Tino cries himself to sleep. It's freezing outside, and he's alone. In the gloom of his poky third-storey bedroom, he can hear pigeons on the window ledge – cooing as they huddle to keep warm. He has been here only two weeks, but already he wishes he were home.

The boat trip from New Zealand had taken four and a half tedious weeks, memorable only for a terrifying storm near Cape Town. On his arrival, Tino went to see his grandmother in the family's old home in the town of Enschede. The sights and smells recalled fragments of his earliest years like a forgotten dream, and immediately he felt comfortable. Too comfortable. In Enschede he was far from the sport he had made the mission of his life – so he caught a train to Amsterdam.

It was like throwing someone from New York into the New Zealand bush. There were so many people. I felt like everything was caving in on me. But I found the house where Johnny Kuiper lived [a Dutch rider who had visited New Zealand two years earlier] and started settling into a new life.

In contrast to Enschede, everything in the large city seemed strange – millions of people packed in like sardines. Tabak had a rudimentary understanding of the Dutch language but couldn't yet string a sentence together. Food and money were scarce; he couldn't just eat when he felt like it, and the meals were minuscule compared with the heaped plates he was used to.

My first meal was like a snack: half a dozen peas, two pieces of carrot and a meatball. That was it. Gone in a scoop. I started sneaking down at night and getting into the fridge.

Hungry, cold and homesick, Tabak might have hopped on the next boat home but for two things: his dream of the Tour de France and his lack of funds. He had just enough money to buy a second-hand racing bike and pay for a few weeks' food and board. To follow his dream, he needed to train, race, win and haul in the prizes – and the need was urgent.

First stop was the RIH bike factory in central Amsterdam. RIH racing bikes were second to none so, naturally, these were the bikes for Tino. They cost a small fortune, but there was one second-hand machine available, Ferrari red, with red handlebar tape and a shiny Brooks leather saddle. It had been raced by the famous Marinus 'Rini' Wagtmans, and with that lineage Tabak was sold on it – 550 guilders, and he rolled it out the door. In a few years' time, the two owners of the red RIH would be riding in the same team.

At last, in the first cold week of January, Tabak was ready to start training. A local bike shop advised that the Windmill Team were the best for training. So, at 9am sharp, Tabak rode out of the city, past people skating along the frozen canals, following snow-lined cycle paths to the designated windmill. There he waited, his white breath punching the freezing air.

Finally, the horizon stirred; a cloud of bike riders was approaching from the city. The formation was four wide, the front eight revolving, like the windmills they were named after. The rest hung on. They flew past without registering the stranger jumping on his red bike and sprinting to catch them – New Zealand's top rider was unable even to hook on to the Dutch training bunch. After half an hour, Tabak gave up, turned around and made his way back to Amsterdam.

I thought, 'Shit! What am I doing here? – cold weather, pigeons keeping me awake, running out of food and low on money.' I couldn't even afford to get punctures.

The following day he returned and – pedals poised – waited. As soon as he saw them coming, he wound it up and hooked on the back – no questions asked, right at the back, on the point of his seat, barely hanging on.

I couldn't believe it! The training there was as hard as the racing. It was absolutely crazy. If there was a crash in training, they wouldn't stop, they'd just go faster. When they were hungry they would take what they wanted from roadside fruit carts. And red lights didn't mean anything.

After two weeks, Tabak could stay just behind the front line – but barely. That's when the others became interested: when they realised he was from New Zealand, and when he was able to hold on. He started to get the knack of their echelon system – the *waaier*. It was just in time, just before his first Dutch race.

It was a Sunday club race in early February. First prize would be a set of wheels, worth two weeks' board. Tabak followed the other riders into the clubrooms as they prepared to get changed. Over their shorts and cycle jerseys, the others pulled on jackets, hats and tracksuit pants. Tino headed to the start line in shorts. Snow still lined the roads. It was bitterly cold. But to his surprise, he found the racing easier than the training. Into the last bend, he was placed second or third. He found himself thinking, *Fuck! I can win this!* And he did. Back in the changing room, all the talk was about the New Zealander with a little bit of Dutch – who had just taken out the big club race.

Next Monday, he was an accepted part of the training group. He made friends and began to pick up the language. That was the start of the giddy, good times. He won two club races from three starts. Dickie, a matchstick of a man from the Windmill Team, gave him a lift in his MG sports car to test his luck in one of the biggest amateur races in Europe.

The Ghent–Ieper (Ypres), a 170-kilometre classic, was the stuff of Tabak's dreams. Everything was thrilling. Most of the competitors were Belgians, born into cycling, hard as nails. Right from the start, Tabak was up the front, ready for the attacks, anticipating the side winds, buzzing with excitement. Then, without warning, the peloton veered on to a small road and sped up. It didn't make sense, there were still 30 kilometres to go at least. Suddenly the course swung left, and there was a wall of cobbles, lined with cheering spectators – the famous Kemmelberg. *No way*, he thought. *That's not rideable!* Hands reached for levers, chains graunched and riders began grinding up the hill.

Pandemonium prevailed. Riders swung to the left, to the right, searching for a better line. The cobbles were wet and slippery. Supporters dashed on to the road. Hands thumped riders on the backside, pushing them up the hill. Tino tried to weave between the madness; he half fell, scrambled to find his footing, shouldered his bike and began to run. On the other side of the road the cobbles turned to smooth concrete – and about thirty riders were forging ahead. He heard those around him panting, 'That's it, no more prizes.' And they stopped.

'Stuff that,' I thought. 'I'm here to race.' So I carried on chasing.

Slowly Tabak hauled in the support vehicles, then the second to front bunch. With the bit firmly between his teeth, he closed on the front bunch – just 25 metres away when the race entered a small village paved with more cobblestones. This time, he was ready. He shifted back on the saddle and cranked down the middle of the road, straight past the whole peloton. The exhilaration gave him power. He was untouchable – and alone.

Soon the lead motorbike was alongside and a voice yelled, 'Thirty seconds [gap].' A little further, it was 70 seconds, with one rider closing – Jos Abelshausen, a Belgian school teacher. Teaming up seemed sensible. Tabak eased the pace, but when the teacher caught up, he told Tabak he was done for; no way could he take a turn. Meanwhile the bunch was gaining, so, after the teacher promised not to sprint on the line, Tabak put his head down and powered on. Twenty metres from the finish line, the well-rested wheel sucker rocketed past.

That was the first time I was conned, and I was gutted. I called him every F-word under the sun, and he didn't even blink an eyelid. It was one of the biggest races. Win that, and you become a professional. I was pissed off and really told him so. But the teacher, he taught me a lesson I never forgot. And people really noticed me. They thought it was amazing.

Those first few months – the winter months – were cold, hungry and hard. Riders wore woollen gloves, balaclavas and knee-high socks over their cycle shoes, with the toes cut away to allow for toe-clips. On bad days, snow and ice settled on clothes, while sweat froze them stiff. Returning from a ride, Tabak would shoulder his bike up three flights of narrow stairs to a small bedroom, turn on the heater, and quickly get changed before laying newspaper on the floor and carefully cleaning every part of his bike.

Then he would rug up and head for the markets to buy bananas and cake, or for a bike shop to buy oil. Everything seemed strange but wonderful. All the busy people, wrapped up tight, calling cheery greetings in their guttural language, long clouds expelled with every breath; the unusual, mouth-watering smells of hot dogs, fish, thick pea soup, coffee and sauerkraut. The markets sold everything his mother had described with such nostalgia.

The Dutch were colourful and confident, compared with the reserved young men Tino had grown up with in rural Canterbury. These people spoke their minds and walked with purpose. Yet the brash Tabak still felt out of place.

Although he had no money, he was reluctant to find a job. His job was cycling – a feeling shared by all serious amateurs across Europe. Riders trained, raced and sold their prizes. The best became professionals. But after a few weeks, Tino, behind on rent, was politely asked to leave his Amsterdam flat. He moved in with a plasterer whose brother was a cyclist. To pay for food and board, he mixed plaster and carried it in bucketloads up narrow stairways. Hard work, indeed, but it meant he had food and a bed.

Seasons moved on, and as the temperature increased, so did the number of races, and with them Tabak's income and popularity.

In some races, especially the amateur classics, you could ride as

When New Zealand track and road champion John Dean toured Europe in 1969 he proved a tough adversary. In the Tour of Twente, a 160-kilometre Dutch amateur classic, Tabak just out-sprinted Dean to take second place. Back in New Zealand, Dean won an astounding 39 national titles. *The Tabak Collection*

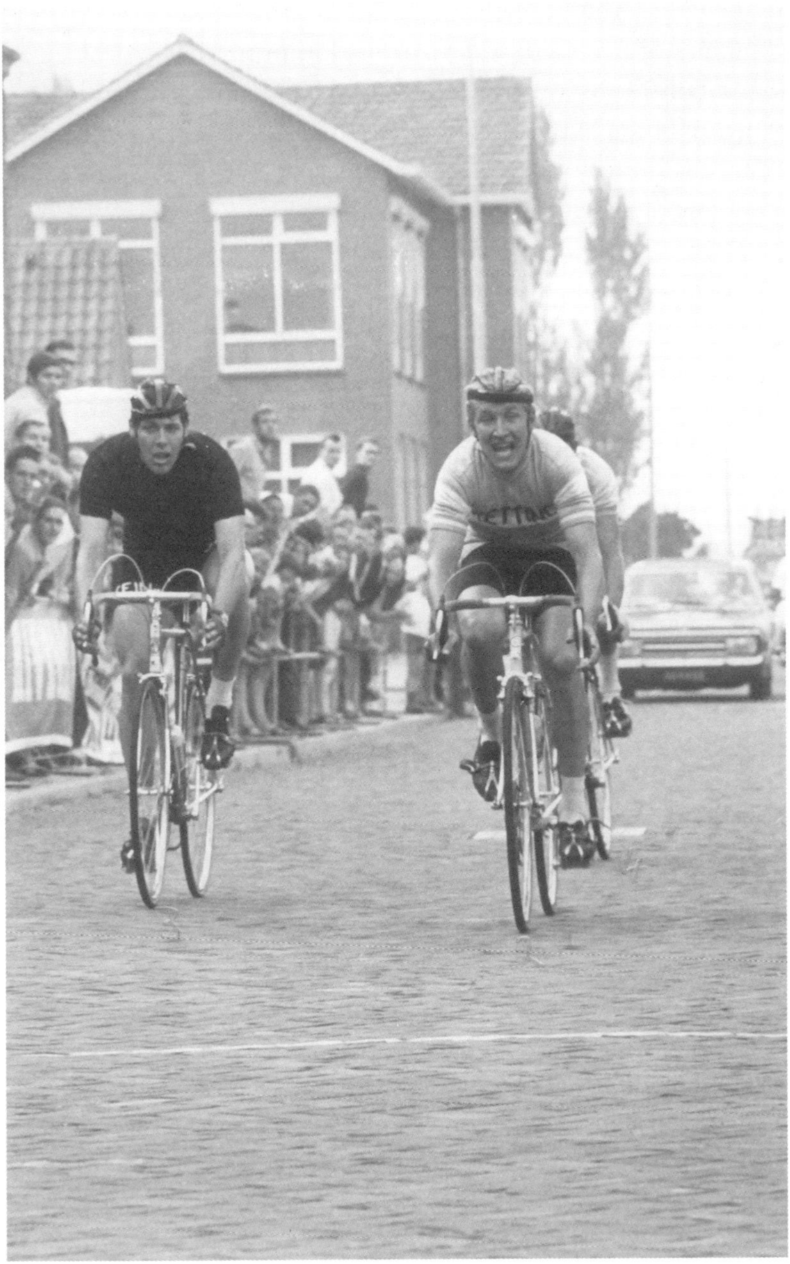

an individual. But generally, riders raced in trade teams; as informal combines of five or six riders; or in club teams. Tabak decided to join a club. There were three or four to choose from in Amsterdam alone, and the Olympia Club, with around 1,000 riders, offered an impressive history of successes. He began wearing the white and red jersey of Olympia.

Then in 1968 the New Zealand Amateur Cycling Association (NZACA) contacted Tabak to offer him a place on the Olympic team heading to Mexico City. But with a hitch: he had to return to New Zealand for Olympic trials. Return home to qualify? He was one of the top amateur cyclists in the world, yet the NZACA still wanted him to jump through hoops. Tabak refused – he didn't have the money anyway. Three days later, Dutch cycling officials offered him a place on the Dutch Olympic team, and within a day he had received a Dutch passport.

I wanted Dutch nationality to get to the Olympics. I didn't feel Dutch. I wasn't Dutch, but I was willing to be Dutch to ride in the Olympics. It was one of the worst decisions I have ever made. End of story!

And it proved to be for nothing: Tino broke his arm in a training race and never made it to the Games. Only two years earlier, when Jentinus (Tino) Tabak and his parents took the Oath of Allegiance at the council chambers in Papanui, the media celebrated. 'Gift from Holland,' they claimed. 'Tino is a New Zealander at Last.' Now that he had renounced his citizenship to join the Dutch cycling team, newspapers recoiled, proclaiming, 'Tino Tabak – Traitor to New Zealand.' His parents were abused and there were threats to burn down their house. Police provided 24-hour surveillance. In the Netherlands, Tino carried on training, oblivious to all the trouble. Obsessed with cycling, he hardly ever wrote or phoned home.

A year later, still in the Netherlands, he was asked to renew his Dutch passport. At the bureau in Alkmaar the grey-haired

Unrequited citizenship? In 1967 this New Zealand magazine clearly welcomed Tabak as a Kiwi. *The Tabak Collection*

official couldn't find his file, until finally she realised, 'Ah, you are a foreigner! That's a different section.'

Still, partial Dutch citizenship was opening other doors. In his second year of European racing, Tabak was accepted into the top rank and was asked to join a combine to compete in lucrative German races. He was soon to learn how successful amateurs survived.

'Clean it up,' *they said and had even arranged who was going to buy the prizes! I didn't understand. Then, as we were getting changed, someone asked, 'Tino, do you want a bit?' By this time, I knew what they were talking about. So I said, 'Yeah, I'll have a bit.' I didn't know what it was, but within a minute, I felt I could walk through a wall and I was talking like a machine gun.*

They say it's bad, but what's bad? It wasn't good, of course. But that day I was in fantasy land and could have taken on the whole world – Arnold Schwarzenegger and Sylvester Stallone combined. I was invincible. When I hopped on that bike, I didn't even feel the pedals, I was in the big gear and ramming away. It worked out so good that I was away on my own, even pedalling around the corners. I crashed on my arse but still felt happy and got up and carried on, covered in blood. We cleaned up. Won all the prizes and sold them.

This was the 1960s, a decade earning itself an indelible reputation for rebellion, free love and drug-altered perceptions, right across society. As with all decades, it was a product of the past. During gruelling Second World War campaigns, British, German and American forces had all been supplied with amphetamines – millions of them. In the following 25 years, 'speed' and other variants of amphetamine were widely used and commonly prescribed. Its best-known descendant, methamphetamine (P), is as common today as speed ever was.

As a performance enhancer, amphetamines had been proved to have a physical effect similar to caffeine, but they also provided a significant psychological boost. Doping in cycling reached the highest levels: former world professional champion Tommy Simpson of Britain died in the 1967 Tour de France with three packets of amphetamines in his back pocket. One pack was empty. Drug testing was in its infancy but suddenly the pressure was on, with the UCI (Union Cycliste Internationale) increasing the number of races that required testing.

In a race in Limburg, south of Holland, our sponsor promised us a car if we won. We were the best amateurs in Holland. I was a good worker, and we had a strong sprinter, who I led up to the finish.

No one knew if there would be testing or not. But if there was, the first three would be tested. This was about the third time that I'd

Tabak on his way to winning a 10-kilometre track race at the Olympic Stadium in Amsterdam in 1969. In third place is John Dean. *The Tabak Collection*

taken anything. It was just what was available, amphetamine again. Halfway through the race, I took one of the pills and felt strong and took the other guy up to the finish line. He won, and I came fourth or fifth, but they called me up for testing anyway.

My mates said, 'Tino, if you drink a lot of milk, they won't find it.' So I hid in the car drinking milk till I was bloated. They called my name over the microphone, and you only have one hour. I went in with five minutes to spare. They told me to pee into a jar. I pretended that I couldn't pee, but in the finish, I gave them a tiny bit.

Two weeks later, the Dutch Cycling Federation came back with results. Tabak was positive. He would be banned from racing for two months.

So they asked if I wanted my second jar tested and it cost 25 guilders per test. I phoned them up and said, 'Don't bother, it will be positive, too.' This was a surprise to them; everyone got their second jar tested and sometimes they were negative. How can that be? I'll tell you. It's because of corruption in some drug-testing circles. Not all – just some. How else could it be possible?

This time I was lucky. When riders in other [European] races tested positive as well, all our test results were mysteriously dismissed. I got a letter from the federation to congratulate me on my sporting efforts and away I went as if nothing had happened. I was quite surprised.

Sometimes riders were given placebos – an injection of vitamins in the backside or a swig of glycerine for the throat – with the aim of providing a psychological boost without the physical effects. For some, the mere belief they had an advantage was enough.

Tabak, centre, in the 1969 World Amateur Team Pursuit Championships in Brno, Czechoslovakia. The Dutch were favoured to win, but failed to place after one of their riders pulled his foot out of his toe-clip at the start.   *The Tabak Collection*

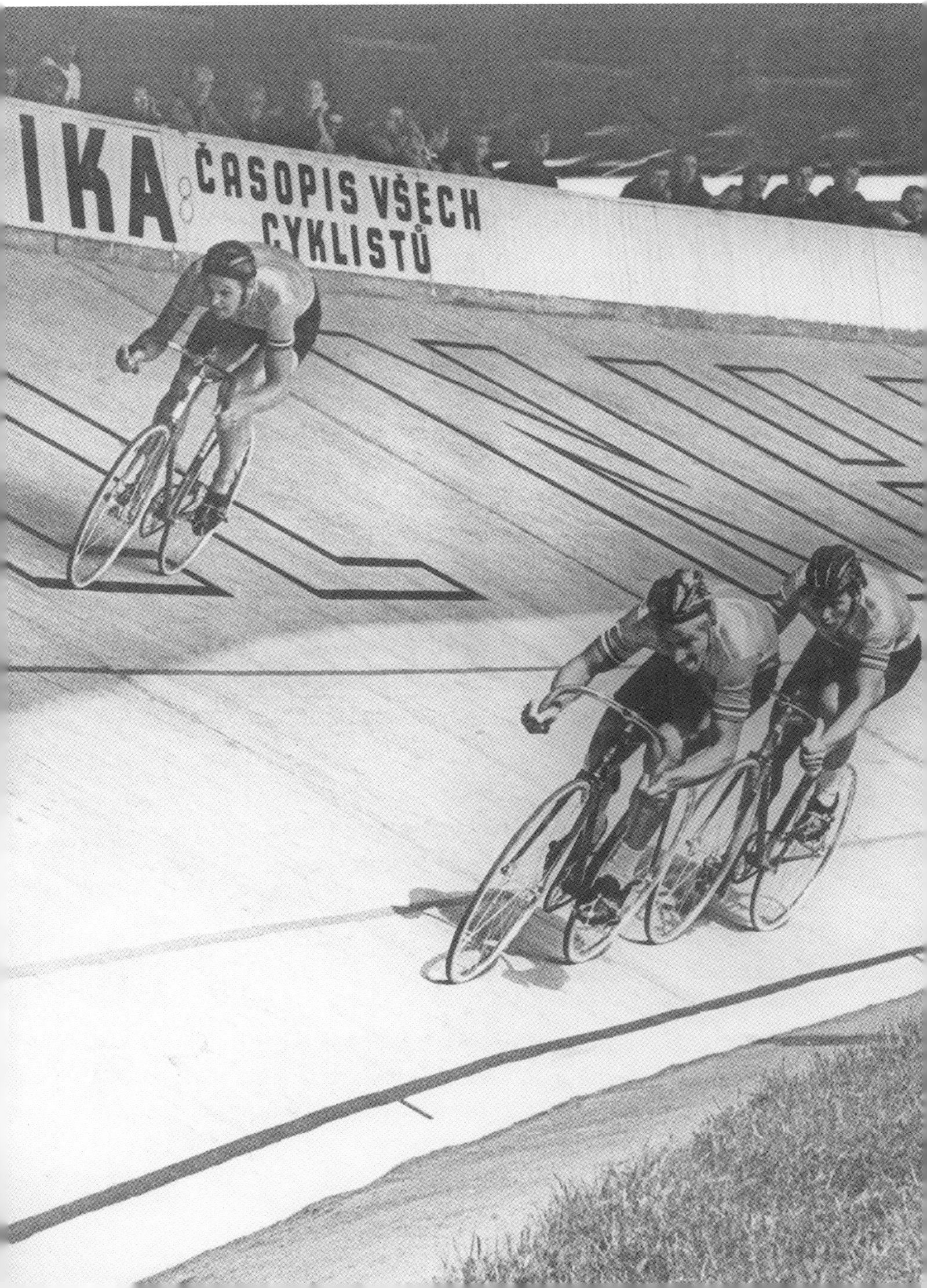
IKA
ČASOPIS VŠECH
CYKLISTŮ

The psychological part of the sport is very, very important: how you can make people just give that little bit more.

'Just that little bit more' was what Tabak always strived for. From 1968 to 1970, he competed in more than 100 amateur races. Despite winning only a few classics and a few criteriums, he rode consistently hard, and stood out as a performer who would attack and break away in every race. It was exactly the racing style the public loved. His combative attributes also made Tabak popular with sponsors, and once established in the Netherlands, he was able to earn good money as an amateur.

Blissfully unaware, he rode into the best phase of his cycling career – and his young adult life. While out for a spin on a cycle path north of Amsterdam he met Mieke Arendsen, a 22-year-old receptionist who loved gymnastics and surf lifesaving. With fine blonde hair and high cheekbones the beautiful Mieke fitted Tino's dreams perfectly. Within weeks they had fallen madly in love and were living together in the seaside village of Egmond aan Zee. The following year, 1970, they married. Relatives from the Netherlands and New Zealand joined many Dutch cyclists in a big celebration. It was the start not only of married life, but also of fatherhood. Mieke had a four-year-old boy called Paul, whom Tino was happy to adopt.

By now Tabak was doing compulsory military training in the Dutch army. Within a short time he had been posted to a special unit of 'sports dropouts' in Amsterdam. Because he was the oldest, he was placed in charge of his barracks. They soon gained a reputation as messy, disorderly, disobedient recruits who would shirk their responsibilities and sneak out of camp at any opportunity. The attempt at military discipline certainly wasn't doing Tino's cycling any harm, though.

In 1970, Tabak achieved the two greatest results of his amateur

In 1970 army cadet Tabak, along with many other sportsmen, was stationed at the barracks in Amsterdam to guard the munitions. *The Tabak Collection*

career. He came third as part of the Dutch team in the 100-kilometre world team trial in Leicester, England. It was, none the less, a bitter disappointment:

Damn it, I've been working towards it [the championships] for three months and I'm only third. It's not good enough!

But a few months later he satisfied himself by winning one of the greatest amateur events, the prestigious Tour of North Holland.

The 168-kilometre classic was a closely fought battle between Tabak and future world champion Hennie Kuiper. They had raced together in the Ketting team and knew each other well, but on this occasion Tabak raced in a military team.

Hennie was a very religious chap, and he always lit a candle before he raced. He got a lot of power out of that. It was a very healthy, clean mind this guy had. He was very, very powerful.

Tabak attacked again and again, and did not appear to be tiring. With 20 kilometres to go, he broke away for the final time and the only rider to stay with him was Kuiper. They quickly got 30 seconds ahead of the peloton and started lapping it out. After three and a half hours in the saddle, Tabak sensed that Kuiper was still riding strongly. He needed an edge.

There is an old rule: to chase is easier than to get away. So with five kilometres to go I said, 'You attack, Hennie, and I'll let you go and we'll just share the prizes if you win.' He was keen, so away he jumped and I pretended that I couldn't stay with him. He was about a lamp post ahead, so I had him in my sights. Just before the finish I got out of my saddle and sprinted him.

The peloton finished only eight seconds behind. After the race Kuiper confronted him with, '*Allez*, Tino, that wasn't very sporting.' Tabak shrugged it off. Winning was what it was all about.

I must have taught Hennie a good lesson, because that never happened to him again, but he did it to others in the professional ranks. His later success really surprised me because he was too kind. Too polite.

The Tour of North Holland was the oldest and biggest amateur classic in the Netherlands. Tabak's victory was not only the peak of his amateur career, it was also the last step in achieving his dream. He was approached by the manager of Mars-Flandria, one of Belgium's strongest professional teams, who offered him a contract to ride with them the following year, 1971. With Mars-Flandria he would be expected to ride all the major classics and tours, including the Tour de France.

Tabak was now a front-of-the-pack amateur, but professional riding was to be something else altogether.

BREAKING AWAY

When I switched to professional racing, there were guys I'd been beating in the amateur ranks leaving me for dead. I thought, 'Hello! What's going on here?'

The fire of Tabak's own ambition and the intense expectations of fans, managers and sponsors made professional racing a pressure cooker – with the heat on full. The season ran from January to October, and the level of competition was unsurpassed. His initiation began with two months of training, and, as the Netherlands winters were so inhospitable, the professionals were sent south to Spain.

At training camp in Spain, in Torremolinos, we were staying in apartments. I heard a noise in the middle of the night and went to the next room. There was a guy high as a kite with his bike in bits on the floor. He was a good bike rider during the day ...

During the day they rode around the lovely Spanish coast and tested themselves in the scenic mountains of the Pyrenees. But this was no holiday: 150–180 kilometres, sometimes more, were covered every day. It provided valuable experience where the flatland cyclists needed it most – climbing and descending. And when they had enough breath to speak, all they talked about was cycling.

In March 1971, racing started. It made little difference that for the first time in his life Tabak was riding a brand new bike, a lightweight twelve-speed Flandria with bar-end shifters and top of the line Campagnolo components. In his debut professional season Tabak struggled just to place in the top ten as he slowly learned the tricks of the trade.

You become professional because you're a good bike rider, of course, but it's got nothing to do with pushing that bike. It becomes a business. If you're contracted to win, you've got to win. Because that's your job – to win. It doesn't matter how you do it.

But if you get contracted to help, then listen mate, you just help. Don't you dare win!

In 1971, Tabak was contracted to help Joop Zoetemelk, leader of the Mars-Flandria team, win the Tour de France. He was so excited he nearly failed the pre-tour medical check – his heart was already racing. As he finally lined up for the greatest race on Earth, alongside the best cyclists in the world, he turned to Zoetemelk and said, 'At last my dream has come true.' He was 25 years old, and the first New Zealander to ride the Tour since Harry Watson in 1928.

The Tour started well. His team, Mars-Flandria, were third in the prologue team time trial. The second day saw three stages, and Tabak placed well in all of them. But it was his exceptional ride on the third day that led him to be proclaimed as 'the revelation of the Tour'. One French newspaper even predicted he would be a threat to Eddy Merckx, winner of the two previous Tours de France.

In Mars-Flandria we had Joop Zoetemelk, who was ready to win the tour, Erik Leman, who was one of the best sprinters, Roger de Vlaeminck, and his brother Erik de Vlaeminck, who was world cyclo-cross champion at the time.

In any case, on the third day, 14 men broke away, with Eddy Merckx, Christian Raymond, Herman van Springel and myself. We were the four people up the front, all giving it hell for leather.

Roger de Vlaeminck was in the break, but Joop had missed out. He was about a minute behind us. So our team manager Briek Schotte drove up and said, 'Allez, Tino!' I said, 'What?' 'You gotta go back and pick Joop up. He's missed the break.' I said, 'Yeah, but I'm here.' He said, 'No, you've got to go back.'

Then Roger de Vlaeminck came up and said, 'Tino, don't.' There was rivalry between him and Joop, even though they were in the same team. So I said, 'Ah well, bugger it. I'm not.' I stuck with the bunch.

Briek came back three or four minutes later, and he ordered me – he actually ordered me – to go back, because I was a helper. I wasn't taken into this team to win the tour.

So I dropped off to the next bunch down. I said, 'Joop, get on my

The world champion Flandria team relaxes with a reporter. To the right of Tabak is world road champion Jean-Pierre Monseré, who died the following month when he collided with a car during a race. Far right is Joop Zoetemelk.   *The Tabak Collection*

wheel.' I actually took him from that bunch back to the leading bunch, and that's where we were. With 15 men.

After 144 kilometres, the stage wound into the magnificent city of Strasbourg on the French–German border. The lead bunch finished as one, with Tabak sprinting in for sixth place. They had averaged an extraordinary 46.6 kilometres per hour and more than eight minutes separated them from the following riders, who were now all out of contention for general classification. Only one of the Strasbourg breakaways could win the tour.

The novice New Zealander – a mere domestique – was now fifth in general classification and was leading the young riders category. But his manager urged him to take it easy. There was still a long way to go – 3,300 kilometres – and Tabak risked hitting the wall.

I started to realise they didn't want me to be a winner. I was a helper. End of story. That pissed me off completely, that I had to look after Joop even though I was riding better than him and was ahead in general classification.

Tino Tabak leading from the legendary Peter Post in a 1971 criterium in the south of Holland. *The Tabak Collection*

It's difficult to fully understand what happened next. At the end of the seventh day, Tabak was eighth in general classification. Looking back now, he believes he became sick after eating an ice-cream. Whatever the cause, on the 221-kilometre mountain stage from Nevers to the massive volcano of Puy-de-Dôme, his legs turned to rubber. He was suffering hot and cold flushes, so a doctor was sent for, who promptly gave him an injection. Two other riders helped him along through the mountain fog; roadside spectators started breaking ranks, taking turns to push him up the hill.

At the top, I could hardly stand. I knew that it was virtually over … What a terrible disappointment.

Tabak finished the eighth stage in last place, 22 minutes behind Luis Ocaña and Joop Zoetemelk. At the end of the next day, halfway through the tour, he pulled out sick, physically and mentally gutted. The dream was over. And Zoetemelk? After two more weeks grinding in the saddle, he finished the Tour ten minutes down; second overall to the Cannibal, Eddy Merckx. On record, it was the fastest race since the Tour began in 1903.

Tabak was lost from the Tour, but not forgotten. He had provided sensational, if grudging, support for his team leader in the critical breakaway of the Tour. He was a colourful rider, often, perhaps too often, to be found forcing the pace at the front of the peloton. Known as 'le blond' in pro circles, he made his mark from the start. The role of domestique had clashed with his natural winner's instinct and doused his excitement at finally riding the great Tour. Soon, though, it would be his turn to play the lion's role and lead a team of his own.

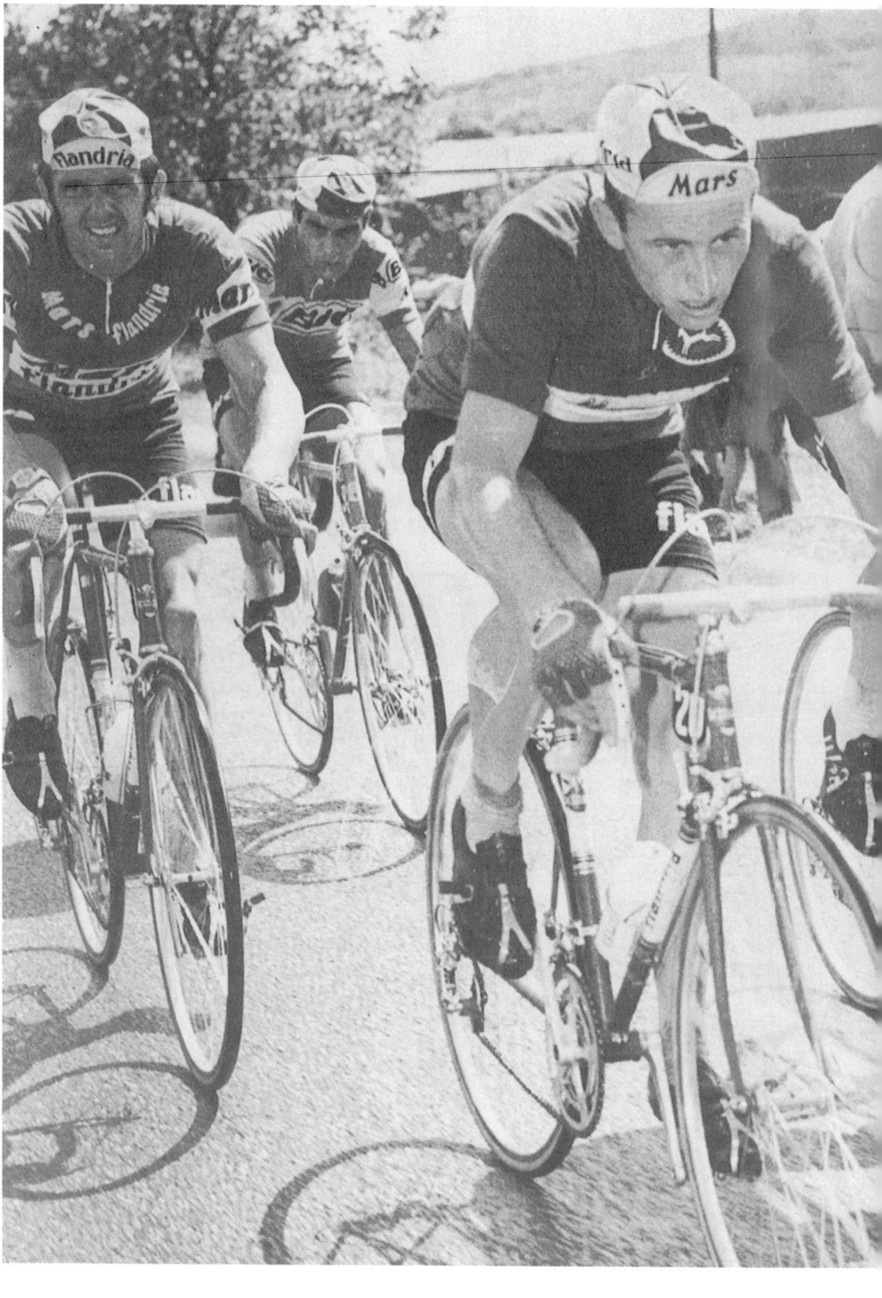

flandria
Mars
Mars flandria

The decisive Strasbourg breakaway led by, left to right, Roger de Vlaeminck, Luis Ocaña, Joop Zoetemelk, Eddy Merckx and Tino Tabak. They averaged 46.6 kilometres per hour in this 144-kilometre stage of the 1971 Tour de France. *Kennedy Brothers, Yorkshire*

A WORLD APART

Every professional sport has its own sort of criminal world.

Tabak had rushed though his apprenticeship; learnt the trade, challenged the stars, and been noticed by those who counted. Now he was granted an opportunity entrusted only to the elite of professional cycling: to lead a team through the great classics, tours and criteriums of Europe. The year was 1972, and the team was Goudsmit-Hoff, who were sponsored by a wallpaper company based in the Netherlands. It was an opportunity all serious cyclists dream of, some aspire to but few achieve. Such a spectacular leap in his career should have propelled Tabak's ambition to even greater heights. Now, he could forget about domestique duties and race solely to win, just as he had always dreamed.

As a helper, Tabak had been expected to protect his leader and follow instructions; no questions asked. Now he had to take control. He had to develop a strategy that would be followed by the whole team. And he had to take the pressure – big pressure. As today, the competition in European racing was intense and public. Media scrutiny was incessant, and there was the immense burden of having to win money for the team.

Naturally, the growing burden of the sportsman was shared by his wife. In an interview with a Dutch magazine, titled 'My Wife Brings Me Bad Luck', Mieke Tabak described how her life was changing:

'Now I am married to a well-known cyclist I can't do so much. In the early days I used to go to all his races, but that doesn't happen any more. Because the cyclists are very nervous before their competition, they react in an unpleasant way towards you. Tino thinks that I stop him concentrating, so he is not very keen that I go with him. But my father goes with him to the races.

'I see other women walking with their men and I am always on my own. I miss that company, especially on my birthday and other festivities. He was away for three weeks for the Tour of Andalucia [Spain], then home for one week, then in France for two weeks before going to Belgium ... and then on to San Remo [Italy].

'If he is home in the weekend he is racing or training five to six hours a day. He has a special diet – no nicotine, alcohol or pork. He has beef steak every day and a crate of oranges a week. Lots of bread, fish and eggs. He weighs 67 kilograms and it must stay at that.

'Tino cleans his bike every day. I'm not allowed to touch it. When he has a new bike he keeps it in the living room. I do all his administration and write all his letters. He can speak Dutch, but cannot write it.

'Sometimes I wonder if our little boy will become a cyclist. He talks about it, but I hope he doesn't because it is such a hard life.'

The 1972 Goudsmit-Hoff team shortly before the Tour de France. Tino is wearing the Dutch champion's jersey. De Pell is on the far left. *Adrian Thornton Collection*

Tabak was still discovering just how hard it could get. Somewhere deep inside, he had already begun to suspect that not only was he unsuited to the role of helper, but he was not a natural leader either. He was a loner — that's why he had taken up cycling in the first place. But in Europe, especially as a leader, knowledge of peloton psychology — how to exploit the peloton's strengths and weaknesses — was essential.

As the season progressed, the responsibility of team leadership began to grind Tabak down. Things came to a head just before the Dutch Professional Road Cycling Championships in June. The opposition was formidable, headed by Joop Zoetemelk, the defending champion. On the eve of the race, the team meeting of Goudsmit-Hoff was one Tabak would never forget.

We had a team manager called Kees Pellenaars [De Pell], and he lined us all up, and told me to stand beside Rini Wagtmans ... He started from the other end, and says to the first rider, 'Listen! Do you want to win tomorrow?' And they said, 'Nah.' Then the next rider, 'Do you want to win?' 'Nah.' He goes right down the line, and then he comes to Rini Wagtmans. 'Rini, do you want to win?' and Rini says, 'Yeah, I want to win tomorrow.' And he had a damn good chance of winning too!

Wagtmans' nickname was 'the White Blaze', and he was renowned as one of the fastest descenders in the world. He had won stages in the tours of France and Spain, as well as several major criteriums. But Rini was starting to suffer from an irregular heartbeat — perhaps he already knew this might be his swansong season.

Rini said, 'I'm prepared to pay 10,000 guilders [NZ$10,000] to the team if they help me to win.' The manager said, 'Okay.' And then he came up to me and he said, 'Tino, do you want to win tomorrow?' I said, 'No, no.' I said, 'I'll take part of the 10,000 guilders Rini's going to give, and I'll do my best for him to win.' Those were my words.

But the manager looked me straight in the eye and said, 'No Tino!

You are going to win tomorrow.' 'But ... I haven't got 10,000 guilders to give.' Again he said, 'You are going to win tomorrow. Don't worry about the money.' And I looked kind of strange at him. He was psyching me up to do things I couldn't do ... In any case, he said, 'That's the end. You all go to bed now.'

That was pure De Pell – a persuasive man who always had a cigar in his mouth. He had publicly stated: 'If Tabak's difficult character gets guided properly, he's capable of doing anything and everything.' And now he was setting out to prove it.

Well, I went to bed, but I didn't sleep. I was just thinking about how I couldn't win because I'd have to pay 10,000 guilders. It was a terrible night. In the morning, I went to the toilet, and this was very weird, a voice said to me, 'Tino, you are going to win. Don't let this uncertainty get the better of you. This is what you want to do.' I was actually talking to myself. And I was thinking how the manager said I was going to win. There was no might win. I pulled the sentence apart, and there were no 'mights', he said I was going to win. 'Right, I'm going out there to win today,' I said. And I sat on the toilet, and I said a prayer. I'm not religious – no way – so don't ask me why, but I actually prayed for enough strength to make me win.

I get to the start, and I see my wife in the stand and give her the thumbs up and away I went. It was a 22-kilometre circuit, and we had to climb the same hill eight times. I'm not a great hill climber, but I've never climbed so fast. It was as if someone was pushing me.

Shortly after the 180-kilometre championship started Rini Wagtmans broke away with four others. His teammate Tabak was not one of them. As soon as Wagtmans had gained two minutes, Tabak attacked with Jan Janssen (the 1968 Tour de France winner) and chased them down. An extra burst, just as Tabak reached the leaders, got rid of Janssen. Wagtmans was also tiring and told Tino

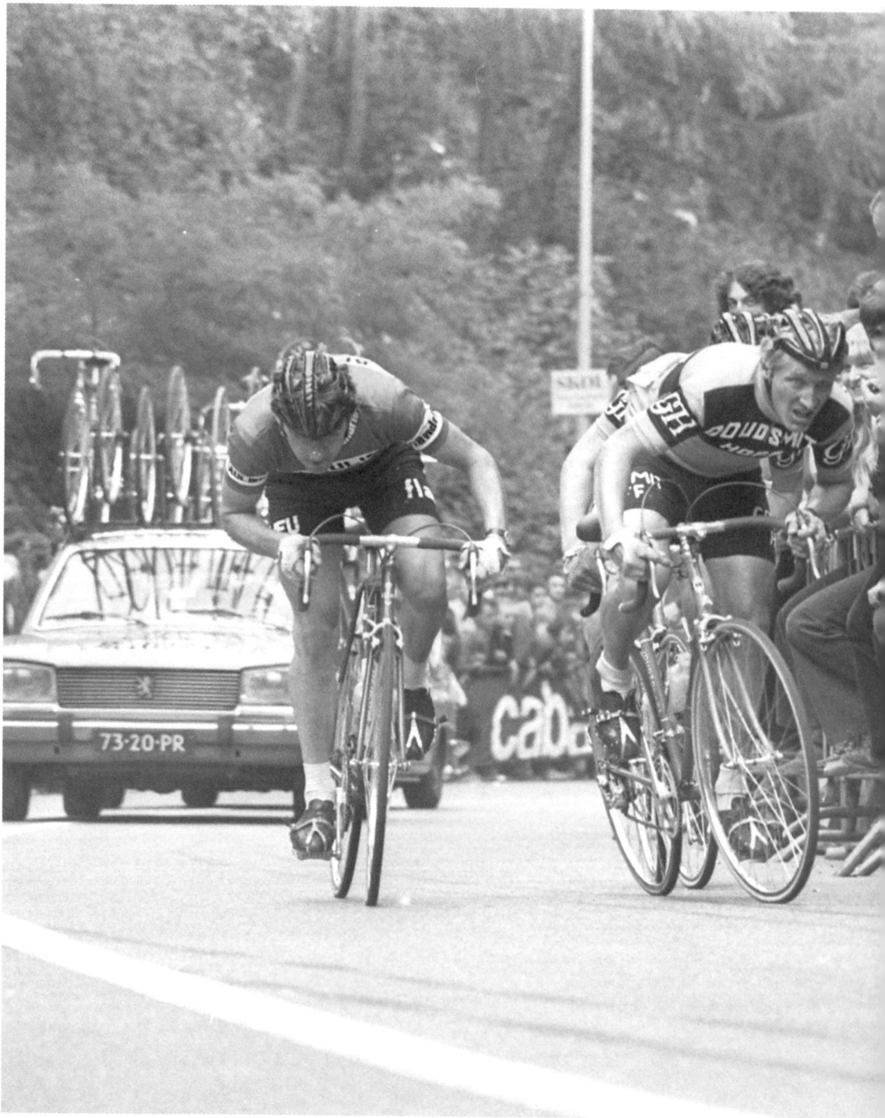
73-20-PR

Around 85,000 spectators watch race leaders Matthijs de Koning, Tino Tabak and Rini Wagtmans (obscured) vie for the title of Dutch professional road champion for 1972.
Netherlands National Library

to attack – 'Become the champion, Tino.' Off he went, like a rocket, but stuck to his wheel was Matthijs de Koning.

De Koning was riding for Joop Zoetemelk, and Zoetemelk, who had started his own counter-attack, was only 1 minute 20 seconds behind – and gaining. Tabak quickly offered De Koning his prize money, and De Koning started helping him along the back part of the course, where there were few spectators to witness the deal.

Zoetemelk was still gaining, so on the second to last climb Tabak took off and rode the last one and a half laps on his own. Forty minutes later he crossed the finish line, with Zoetemelk in second place, just under a minute behind.

It was like a dream. I had taken out the Dutch championships! But I wasn't strong enough to handle all that. Mentally I wasn't ready for it. It was far, far too much. The whole professional world is crazy. It was actually getting at me. Driving me crazy. From then on, I had to win races 'cause I was Dutch National Road Champion.

THE SPECIAL TRICK

The 1972 Tour de France started a week and a half later. As with all the top riders in the 1970s, Tabak was scheduled to race around 110 days that year, including several major tours. But the Tour de France was then, as it is today, the greatest and toughest annual sporting event in the world. The pressure cranked up again.

Goudsmit-Hoff raced the Tour with 11 riders. They had two vehicles and three spare bikes. Backing the riders were the manager, two mechanics and two soigneurs.

The manager, De Pell, picked team members and co-ordinated

Tino and Mieke on the podium after the 1972 road championships. *The Tabak Collection*

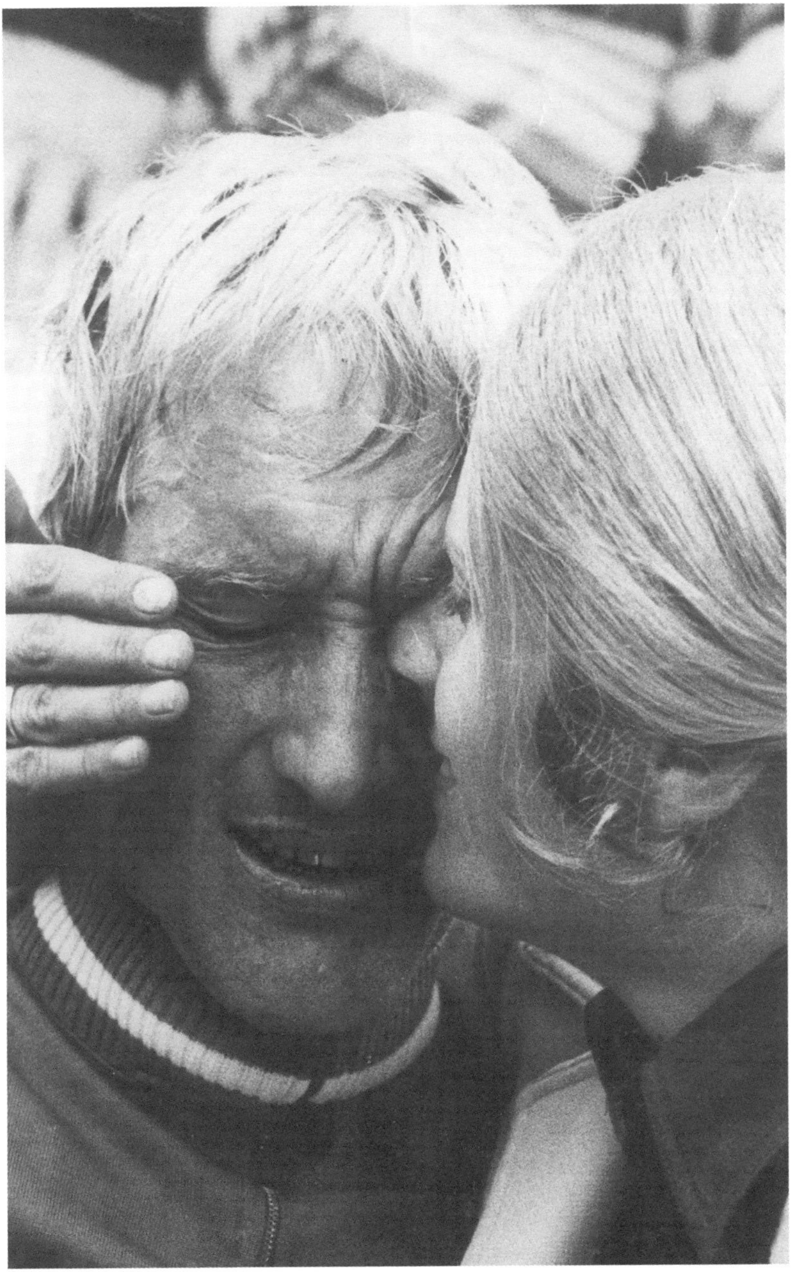

the team. De Pell followed the peloton in a car, with the mechanics packed in the back, constantly jostling for position with all the other team cars. There were no radios or cellphones in those days. Messages were passed between the team car and the riders by hand signals and shouting. If it was top secret, sometimes notes were passed on in a bidon (drinking bottle).

The mechanics were the most reliable, solid members of the team. *They were the only sane ones in the whole profession, and their job was a lot harder than people realised.*

After a day of bad weather, the mechanics would begin a race of their own, taking the bikes to bits and repacking all bearings, checking tyres, truing wheels in preparation for the next day's riding. They concentrated their efforts on the bike that belonged to their leading rider and might be found working outside under a tarpaulin until the early hours.

Then there were the soigneurs. These men did everything else ... *Soigneurs were like sleazy little witch doctors. They weren't criminals, but they were on the edge, always trying to look for something to make their rider go better. They had a lot of prestige. They would compete among each other, to say they were the world's best. Looking back now, they were absolute nutters, but they were also a lot of fun, and they did give you the inspiration. They had this charisma and gave you morale, with awesome massages and pep talks.*

They would prepare you for the following day in their own personal little ways, and they all had their own preparations [of medication], which they carried around in a special suitcase that nobody but them was allowed to touch.

The Molteni team would empty their rubbish bins when they left a hotel just because they didn't want other soigneurs to go into their rooms and check their rubbish, which they did! ... It wasn't so much that Molteni were on anything – their riders were so good, they probably weren't — but the other soigneurs had to find out what they could.

Before a big race, they could give you the 'truc special', the 'special trick'. They had all sorts of ointments and pills, and would take all the labels off, so no one knew what it was. It might have been sugar pills but they made it something special just by telling you it was special.

They'd say, 'Your legs feel so good. You're going to fly today.' Then you'd ask, 'Have you got something special for me?' and they'd say, 'Oh yeah.' And they'd go to their secret suitcase and get you something, whatever, and if you asked what it was they'd give a wink and say, 'Ah, no, no, no ... you'll go all right today.'

Often soigneurs would be up until well after midnight and would rise again hours before the race start, preparing the riders' food, bidons, and clothes. The food varied from rider to rider: Tino liked bananas, cakes, apples, rice cakes and Mars bars. All the food

Wagtmans, De Pell and Tino at the 1972 Dutch championships. *Netherlands National Library*

was cut up and carefully wrapped in individual paper parcels that could be opened easily while cycling.

Many of the hotels along the race routes lacked hot showers or clothes dryers, and each day the soigneurs would be obliged to wash the riders' clothes as best they could, starting, of course, with the top riders. If the weather had been bad, slower riders could expect dirty, damp clothes for the next day's racing.

Le Tour was a man's world. Women – even wives – were barred from the hotels. At the end of a stage, one soigneur might be there to direct weary riders to their accommodation where the other had prepared buckets of warm water for bathing if there were no baths or showers available. Sometimes there would be a flask of warm tea and a cake waiting for them. If it was cold, exhausted riders would sleep in their tracksuits with their caps on.

One hundred and thirty-two racers – representing 12 teams – began the 59th Tour de France. They faced 3,846 kilometres over 20 stages. This was Goudsmit-Hoff's first and last Tour de France. Tabak, the anxious leader, bearing the weight of the red, white and blue Dutch national champion's jersey, was more stressed than ever and took sleeping pills to avoid lying awake at night dwelling on the next day's stage.

I could follow a break, if I didn't miss it of course, but I wasn't strong enough in my mind to create a break or make a decision. That was getting me down. I struggled with it, in every stage.

The stresses of leading a team would be temporarily surpassed by epic mountain stages, such as the Col du Tourmalet (2,115 metres) and the Col du Galibier (2,556 metres). Both are far bigger than any mountain road in New Zealand.

[In the mountains] you would dread the moment when the climbers start attacking. Just hanging in with the front bunch, hoping they won't attack and split the field early. If they wait and wait, then it just happens later.

The route of the 1972 Tour de France.

It's hot – tar is melting on the road. You're not drinking much, because you're still in the bunch, still busy. Then all of a sudden these idiots start attacking you left, right and centre, 'cause they're going for the mountain prizes. And you're on the point of your seat, swaying left and right. You try changing gears, and everything, but then it's over – they're gone.

You form your own little group then, and you get to know those riders over time. And accept it. You get in a rhythm and try to keep it, for an hour or more, all the way to the top. I was better than the average climber. But I wasn't the best.

I didn't mind the downhills. They can be scary when they're wet, but if you're having a good day you don't think about crashing.

That year there were eight mountain stages of between 150 and 220 kilometres, and Tabak's inconsistent performances on the climbs steadily eroded his position on general classification. On the flat stages he was able to stay with the main peloton, but in the mountains he finished between one and 13 minutes behind the stage winners. The 207-kilometre Mont Ventoux stage was typical. The winner was Bernard Thévenet, with a time of 7 hours 13 minutes. Tabak was five minutes back. Out of the 100-odd riders still contesting the tour, he placed 21st and won the daily prize for the Most Elegant Rider. There were several daily prizes, which ensured that every team got their share of the limelight and kept their sponsors happy.

Keeping the sponsors happy was foremost in De Pell's mind. From the outset of the Tour, he manoeuvred his team into whatever position would gain Goudsmit-Hoff publicity. If television cameras were filming, he might order his riders to the front, and if other teams got the same order the peloton speed would go from 30 to 50 kilometres per hour. Of course some riders were allocated to help Tabak by collecting water, or providing support after a puncture, but others were instructed to try to win a stage at all costs, even if it meant they were then too exhausted to continue. More than half the team would not reach Paris.

They made plenty of attempts, placing in the top ten several times, but a stage win eluded them. Near the end of the Tour, the cunning De Pell arranged one last attack. Rini Wagtmans was so far out the back on general classification that he posed no threat to the Tour leaders. This was also his last racing season. Perhaps, as a farewell gift, they would let him go and take a stage. And what a stage. From Belfort to Auxerre, the 257-kilometre stage 18 was the longest in the Tour and would take well over seven hours. They had only just left the mountains behind and wanted to recuperate before the grand

Pour ceux qui n'aiment pas...

The caption that went with this photo read: 'Here's how a rider in the Tour de France gets an injection. One can't tell who to admire more, the rider (in this case Wagtmans), or the doctor, who is working here at 40 kilometres per hour on the Route des Princes d'Orange.'
Adrian Thornton Collection

finale in Paris. The Tour rode as one, an iridescent peloton flowing across the French countryside at a steady 33 kilometres per hour.

After several hours, at an agreed point, the remains of the rookie Dutch team attacked. Tour leaders – Eddy Merckx, Raymond Poulidor, Felice Gimondi – simply watched them go. Wagtmans tucked in behind his teammates Tabak and Gerard Vianen who forged ahead, exhausting themselves and eventually dropping back to be swallowed by the peloton. But they had done their job brilliantly and won the daily award for Teamwork, a scooter that was sold back in Holland. Rini Wagtmans had the lead he needed and crossed the line alone, against a backdrop of the 85 riders finishing 20 seconds behind him. It was the final victory of his career and a fine result for Goudsmit-Hoff.

Eighty-eight weary riders rolled into Paris a few days later. After a month on the road, Tabak came 18th in the 1972 Tour de France, an hour behind the invincible Merckx. This remains by far the best result for a New Zealander. But what did this mean for a man who only wanted to be number one?

Was I disappointed at coming 18th? I sat down on a stool at the finish at the Parc des Princes and they told me that I was 18th. I got 18th … That says it all. Could have done better.

Tabak completed at least four other tours that season, placing as high as third overall in the Tour of Levant and infuriating other top riders by attacking so much. Felice 'The Phoenix' Gimondi, who placed second to Merckx in the Tour de France, told a reporter: 'If I had Tabak's legs I'd win a hell of a lot of races.' Despite the best efforts of those legs, however, a stage win still eluded Tabak – though he had more success in criteriums.

The Netherlands' most prestigious criterium was the 100-kilometre Acht van Chaam, held in the village of Chaam a week or two after the Tour de France. There were rich prizes and, that year,

85,000 spectators. With his team blocking the field, Tino broke away with only a Luxembourg rider sticking to his wheel. Whether he needed it or not, he decided to buy security.

Slowly you get into this system of having to buy races. Now what I mean by buying races is buying security. I was away with the Luxembourg rider, who I could probably beat, but I didn't know if he could sprint – and I've got to win, for my sponsor. So I said, 'I'll give you $1,000 if I win.'

He accepted. *So then I had security. It doesn't mean you definitely will win, because he could still double-cross you, but it improves your chances. And I did win the Acht van Chaam that year. You would have to be very confident not to buy security. It was normal. Make an offer and expect a yes or no answer. You've got to be good to make this sort of deal – and still ride well at the finish, or it'll backfire on you.*

Arranging victories only happened between top riders who were fairly evenly matched. *You don't do deals with a donkey!* As Freddy Maertens explained in his biography, 'Anyone who thinks he can win a race will have a go, but if he's not sure about it, he pays out to make sure. That's the way it is. On our licences it says we are *professional* riders.' Conversely, if a rider thought they were going to lose anyway, they would naturally be inclined to accept a little extra pocket money. But to play the game, you had to be a threat. Clearly Tabak was respected, although team leadership hardly led to the dream run he'd fantasised about. Through 1972 he climbed the podium for three wins, one second and two thirds. Racing in the Dutch champion's jersey gave him a high market value, resulting in lots of publicity and a reasonable wage – 20,000 guilders plus appearance money of up to 500 guilders per start. Then disaster struck. At the year's end the company director of Goudsmit-Hoff died. His replacement had no interest in cycling, and the team was disbanded.

Tino's time as a team leader had come to an end, and he was in no hurry to repeat it.

THE SUB-TOPPER YEARS

It's just like a dream. One minute you're in Holland: the next, you're back where you started bike-riding. Everything has to have a foundation and this country is the foundation of what I have done in cycling. But don't forget, a lot said I was mad when I went to Europe – but a lot of them aren't riding any more and I am, professionally. (1972 interview with Tino Tabak)

As an isolated but wealthy nation, New Zealand had a long tradition of importing overseas champions to compete against local heroes. Major Taylor, Plugger Bill Martin, Arie van Vliet and Reg Harris had all entertained Kiwi crowds, but never before had a New Zealand champion gone overseas and returned as one such challenger.

In the summer of 1972–73, it was Tino's biggest fan – Gerben Tabak – who arranged a tour of the country from Auckland to Invercargill for the Dutch professional champion. But this was not the only reason the tour was exceptional. Most notably, the Amateur Cycling Association bent over backwards to get a slice of the action. It made the unprecedented move of passing a special ruling to allow its amateur riders to race against Tabak. Amateurs were sworn never to race against the 'cashies' and for most this would be the first and last time they ever did so. It showed the association believed its riders had risen to world class and would not be embarrassed by a European professional. Of course it helped that January was the height of the New Zealand track season and Tabak was only just starting to train for the European road season.

The Tabak tour, which was sponsored by Coca-Cola, was the last time he raced in New Zealand. In between events he was out on the road, clocking up hundreds of miles a week. To ride from Christchurch to Timaru before starting an evening of track events was typical. On the track he was pitted against all the top contenders, alternating between 'cashies' and amateurs, including Olympians John Dean, Neil Lyster and Robert Oliver. Naturally, in the shorter events Tabak finished with the field, but he showed his class in any race more than 20 minutes long. In a 40-lap points race in Palmerston North he was reported to be 'an easy winner in the final and toughest event of the day'.

The tour also provided an opportunity for his wife Mieke to visit the small country that she had heard so much about. In the back of Tino's mind he always hoped to return, but their trip failed to convince Mieke that New Zealand was the paradise he had described. It wasn't so much the backward culture, the grating accents, or the bad coffee, but Mieke was a 'village girl'. Like many small towns in Holland, Egmond aan Zee was close-knit – parochial even. It virtually had a dialect of its own, distinct from the other unique towns just five kilometres to the north and south. Mieke had grown up in the village and was definitely not leaving its familiar sights and sounds and people for a strange little country at the end of the world.

Back in Europe, the racing season started with a duel against the exceptional Spanish rider Luis Ocaña, in the Grand Prix de Menton. Hammering over the mountains on the south-east border of France, Tabak was on fire. Looking back, he presumes he'd done more training than Ocaña and the track racing in New Zealand had put some speed into his legs, for on that day he rode him out of his wheel. They were miles ahead of the rest. Still, Tabak made an arrangement to assure victory.

You always had to perform. The pressure never stopped, and it drove some riders mad. In New Zealand there was only one Tino Tabak and I was the best. In Europe there were 500 Tinos, and we lined up beside real legends like Merckx, Poulidor, Ocaña and Zoetemelk.

It gives you goose bumps to ride beside Merckx, or Poulidor. Those guys were special. If they said jump, we all jumped. If the Molteni team wanted a toilet break, they could arrange it and the whole bunch stopped. It was absolute dog weather once, in the Tour of Belgium. We were all struggling, like zombies. All of a sudden I saw Eddy Merckx in front of me, and his bike was shaking. I saw him stop! That was the sign for me to stop, too. I thought, 'If he is suffering that much, then I should stop now.' People came to put blankets around me and silver paper. We abandoned the race.

A few months later, Tabak again broke away with Ocaña, on the ultimate race – the Tour de France. It was 1973; the Spaniard was destined to win. Tabak was racing for Sonolor, a mainly French team that looked down their Gallic noses at him. Friction was inevitable.

Sonolor's 1973 Tour de France team. Tino is third from right. *The Tabak Collection*

With 15 kilometres to go, I broke away with Ocaña and one of his teammates, then at two kilometres I broke away from them. But near the finish, my own teammate sprinted up with the bunch and passed me. I was so angry that the next day I just attacked, attacked, attacked, right from the beginning until I hit the wall. We never got on after that.

But, for Tabak, the horrors of the 1973 Tour had only just begun. On stage eight, he reached the Col du Galibier six minutes down and chased furiously down the other side. In his book *Rugnummers en Ingevette Benen* (Backnumbers and Liniment-Rubbed Legs), Dutch broadcaster Mart Smeets provides a vivid eyewitness account.

'During the descent of the Galibier he crashed close to a big ravine and was spread-eagled on the ground. I was driving that day behind the bunch and saw Tabak crash. Because the Tour keeps going, it doesn't stop; Tabak had to keep going with all the pain that he was having ...

'Luis Ocaña was [stage] winner, and Tabak was more than an hour behind. And he still hadn't come in. Then all of a sudden he came into view ... a very sad heap of human being.

'Tabak was crying and covered in blood. His leg was open from the hip to the ankle – he looked like a piece of steak. And we could see stones in the wounds. Gently we lifted him off his bike and tried to find a doctor. We looked for the soigneur of the team – couldn't find him either. He sat on the ground next to his bike. It looked like a piece of art; the steering and the wheels were all crumpled in together. There we were standing. Everyone had gone home. There was nobody. The streets were empty. And he was forgotten.

'We decided to carry Tino to the car, and drove at top speed to the village and found the school where the Sonolor team were staying and there we dropped him off. The soigneur was busy all night taking stones out of the wounds. Later we heard that nobody was interested in him any more. And that's how the tour goes.

Crash – a pity. Injured – go home. He got a nod from the team and that's all he got. It was finished. He could go back to Holland. The tour must go on.'

'TINO'S STATION ON THE CROSS' was how one newspaper headline described it. A spread of photos showed the doctor leaning out of a convertible, examining his wounds; Tabak's face contorted with agony; a sympathetic spectator running beside him, offering to push with a hand on his injured hip and Tabak 'screaming like an animal' to be left alone.

I can remember now how I crashed and the team manager put me on the bike again. The tour doctor drove beside me, cut open my ripped shorts and gave me an injection. Then later my bike just collapsed on me.

Even after such a terrible crash, Tabak would not stop. The Tour doctor examines his injuries from the support vehicle. *The Tabak Collection*

You still try to go on. I got up and put my steering straight. My front wheel had a big buckle in it. I tried to straighten it, then undid the clip on my brake. Got someone to help me back on my bike and rolled down the rest of the Col du Galibier. I couldn't move my left hand.

At the finish line, there was no sign of the Tour. Everything had been taken away to the next stage. After 8 hours 55 minutes' riding, Tino finished last in 107th place. It was extraordinary he had finished at all.

The TV crew dropped me off at the school barracks and said, 'Here's Tabak.' No one cared. Years later it sank in, and I thought, 'Fuck yous.' We were sometimes treated like absolute crap, and when I think back now, it sort of disappoints me. We were worthless if we weren't riding well.

In cases like this, they sent you home because you cost them money. I never had no telephone call or anything to see how I was getting along – and I never got paid.

After such a promising start to the season, the crash had a devastating effect. At hospital, X-rays revealed a fractured hip, possibly forcing an early retirement. Resting up at home, with Mieke providing as much support as possible, Tino slowly healed, but with no racing his finances and morale suffered. He stopped wearing a gold ring he had won as 1966 Canterbury Sportsman of the Year, believing its mojo had run out.

In September, the birth of his daughter, Melanie, temporarily lifted his spirits; then the worries about money and cycling swamped him again. There was no professional cyclists' union and riders had virtually no rights. Tabak's contract with Sonolor simply stated, 'We will prolong your contract if your results are satisfactory.' Right now, though, in the autumn of 1973, Tabak's mind was spinning with all the desperate options for breaking free from whatever it was that was holding him back.

I was in the jungle category, the in-betweens, the sub-toppers. I wanted to be in the Merckx category but I wasn't. I definitely didn't want to be in the category below me, but was, and so I struggled to get above it and couldn't accept it. Sub-toppers. Almost there and almost not. It's a dangerous category. It's like having a dream, where you're trying to get away from someone, but you just can't quite make it. Just sort of knocking on the door of the top riders, but the door isn't opening. That puts you in the category of ... going to the extreme.

If I had obviously been in the lower category, I would have known my job was a helper, and I would have just accepted it. But me being me, I knew – I know – that I could have, and I should have, done better.

One of the first big races Tabak attempted after recovering from the crash was the Grand Prix d'Orchies in northern France. This was an end-of-season classic, about 200 kilometres long, undulating, with cobbles in the last hour. Most of the good riders were there, and Tabak was fresh. So he attacked early and built up several minutes' lead.

I was on the edge of succeeding, but I knew I had to do something. I had to win a big race to continue. So I did something – but did it too much.

I was away on my own and had five or six minutes, when I hit the cobblestones. I hadn't eaten enough, and I just blew to the world. It's as if you're drunk and someone's trying to wake you up. I was shaking and my head was going left and right. I had a dry mouth and legs like rubber. By the time the peloton caught me, I was so far gone.

I remember crossing the finish line, somehow getting to the showers and then collapsing ... Later, when my wife found me, I was still sitting on the shower floor with water running over me. She said, 'Are you all right, Tino?', and I told her, 'If anything happens to me, this is what I did ...' She said, 'You silly man.'

I'd taken a cocktail of all sorts of shit [painkillers and stimulants] before the start and every 20 minutes during the race. Because I had to win.

Cost? What cost? I had to win to go further. But at the end, I actually thought I was going to die. My whole body was trembling. My head was like a massive hangover. Sick in my stomach – empty, white as a ghost, blurry vision, heart going a thousand beats a minute. That was a big risk, and I think it was almost the end of my cycling.

But I didn't want to work – work scared the shit out of me. There was nothing beyond cycling – didn't even think about other things. So I carried on cycling.

Some men learn from books, others by experience. Tabak had no qualifications, and little formal education, but his experiences and knowledge, both good and bad, of professional racing at world-class level had taken him far beyond any other New Zealander.

People say taking drugs is cheating. Of course it's cheating, but cheating for what? Money? Fame? I was a keen, green New Zealander; I didn't know anything. I grabbed at the wrong things. Was it right? Was it wrong? Some people don't like hearing it. Tough! It's what happened. In everything where people strive to achieve things, they will do anything to get to the top. But in cycling, testing for certain things became a witch-hunt.

Tino looked around him and observed double standards between cycling and other high-ambition pursuits in search of performance enhancers. Bottled oxygen to assist climbers beyond the 'death zone' to the summit of Everest. Cosmetic surgery to extend slumping supermodels' careers. Amphetamines to help the US military fight harder. Caffeine, strong coffee or pills to stimulate driven businessmen. Tabak, like many riders, could not help but make these comparisons.

Ethical and health issues aside, one thing was clear – the moral goalposts, as ever, were shifting. Not only for cycling, but for sport in general.

Eddy Merckx, Joop Zoetemelk, Freddy Maertens – countless stars as well as water carriers – were tainted as drug testing evolved. According to European cycle historian Les Woodland, most top riders – amateurs and pros – took medication: 'It has been that way all along. If the choice is between painting walls or labouring in the fields or chiselling coal and living your dream of bike racing, why hesitate if the only condition is that you take what everyone else is taking?'

Yet increasingly sponsors and supporters (especially rivals' supporters) demanded moral as well as physical superhumans. Jacques Anquetil rebelled, claiming that professional cyclists were workers and had the right to treat themselves as they wished. The five-time Tour de France winner famously finished one interview with: 'Leave me in peace; everyone takes dope.'

Tabak was in a jungle that made amateur cycling back home, for all its bureaucratic rules and petty arguments, seem like a cyclists' utopia. In Europe, blindfolded by ambition, he had ridden himself into a quagmire and was now stuck there, thrashing around for another victory. Luckily – maybe unluckily – there was one man who would provide him with the opportunities he sought.

RALEIGH'S CAPTAIN

Peter Post, the Emperor of the Six Days, had finally retired. Claiming victory in the 1964 Paris–Roubaix and the 1965 Dutch road championships was of little note compared with his record 65 six-day track race wins. Now the famous Dutchman intended to satisfy his ambition vicariously.

In 1974, Post set up the first professional team sponsored by the colossal English cycle manufacturer TI-Raleigh. Against Post's wishes, Raleigh insisted that some English riders be included. To bridge the gap between Dutch and English, a strong bilingual rider was needed: enter Tino Tabak. Now, Post was a hard man. And as a former champion experienced in all aspects of cycling, he was one of the few authority figures who commanded Tabak's respect. Post recognised that Tabak was, as one reporter put it, 'somewhere between a star and a domestique'. Knowing that Tabak would be unhappy riding as either a leader or a helper, he appointed him as a 'captain' to assist with team communication. Post also encouraged him on his solo escapades.

Post had attracted enough sponsorship to provide good pay and conditions for his riders. Tabak responded to the security.

The untested Raleigh Team made their debut on 16 March 1974 in the 200-kilometre Tour of South Holland, which started and finished at The Hague. They won the team prize and Tabak finished third out of 150 pros. The very next day Tabak entered another 200-kilometre race, the Circuit of Kemzeke in Belgium, and won. Back in the saddle only 48 hours later, and he won the Omloop van het (Circuit of) Waasland. It was a spectacular start for Raleigh and in May the *Telegraaf*, Holland's biggest newspaper, awarded the prestigious Telesport Trophy to Tino Tabak.

On paper at least, 1974 was his best racing year; he won eight races (mostly criteriums) and placed top ten in more than twenty. Some were big classics, others smaller events in England. Standout results included a fourth place in the venerable Tour of Belgium and eighth in the Amstel Gold Race, a 238-kilometre Dutch classic. Post was pleased and offered another contract for 1975. Again the year was set to go well, but conflict flared when Tabak entered a big Dutch criterium, the Acht van Chaam.

Raleigh had not entered a team in the Tour de France that year, so the race organisers placed Tabak in the B grade. He was infuriated, went to the papers, and argued that as he had won the same criterium in 1972 he should definitely be in the A grade. The organisers recanted, but this last-minute change meant Tabak was unable to get into any combines. Why? French rider Erwann Menthéour explains: 'The script of a criterium is written in advance. The first two places are shared out according to the placings in the Tour, the most popular riders in the race, and to the local champion, who's given the right to show himself off.' Gatecrashers were not welcome. Tabak would have to stay at the front and watch like a hawk for any breakaways.

Joop Zoetemelk suddenly swerved to the right and attacked. No one reacted. It was a narrow bit of road and his team had completely blocked it, but not before I managed to break away. It all happened in seconds. I realised that Joop was a combine leader, and it was his turn to win.

I had to get on his wheel. There was so much hassle for me to get in A grade, I was absolutely pissed off. Now I was in the break, and I wasn't going to let him get away.

Then one and a half laps from the finish, we started talking about who was going to win. I said, 'Okay Joop, I want to win this. I'll give you 1,000 guilders plus my prize.' He said, 'No, no, no, I'll give you 500.' I said, 'Well, that doesn't work, does it?' But that's what he insisted on, so I thought, 'Stuff you.'

Up till then I'd been taking turns and working real hard. You can't just sit on someone; the crowd certainly don't accept that sort of rubbish. It's really, really hard racing. So we were both getting knackered. But we couldn't agree about the way it goes, so for the last three-quarters of a round I just sat on his wheel. I thought, 'That's it. I'll get him.' He didn't want to slow up because the main bunch would catch him, but he did slow up in the last one and a half kilometres to make me take a turn. And the bunch did start catching up.

Near the finish, the crowd started screaming, 'Joopy, Joopy, Joopy!' because he was the local hero. It was a cobblestone finish. The race commentator went '... and you can see them coming round the corner; and Joop's in the lead; and Joop's going to win. Joop's going to win – and – ah – and here comes Tino! Tino Tabak! Tabak wins!'

Now, it was so close, I don't know who was first. You couldn't see on the photos. Could have been Joop. But because the speaker said, 'Tabak wins', I won the race. I was on cloud nine. I'd really showed them I was an A-grade rider. I got a flower wreath, and then all of a sudden it was, 'Tino, Tino, Tino!' That's how it works. You're a hero when you're in the winning move. When you're not winning, you're a nobody.

I went to collect my prize and it wasn't there! I was told, 'No, no, it's already been arranged.' I said, 'What's fucking been arranged?' And they said, 'We took you into the combine.' I was furious. My prize money paid for Joop's combine. But you can't really do anything because it's all secret.

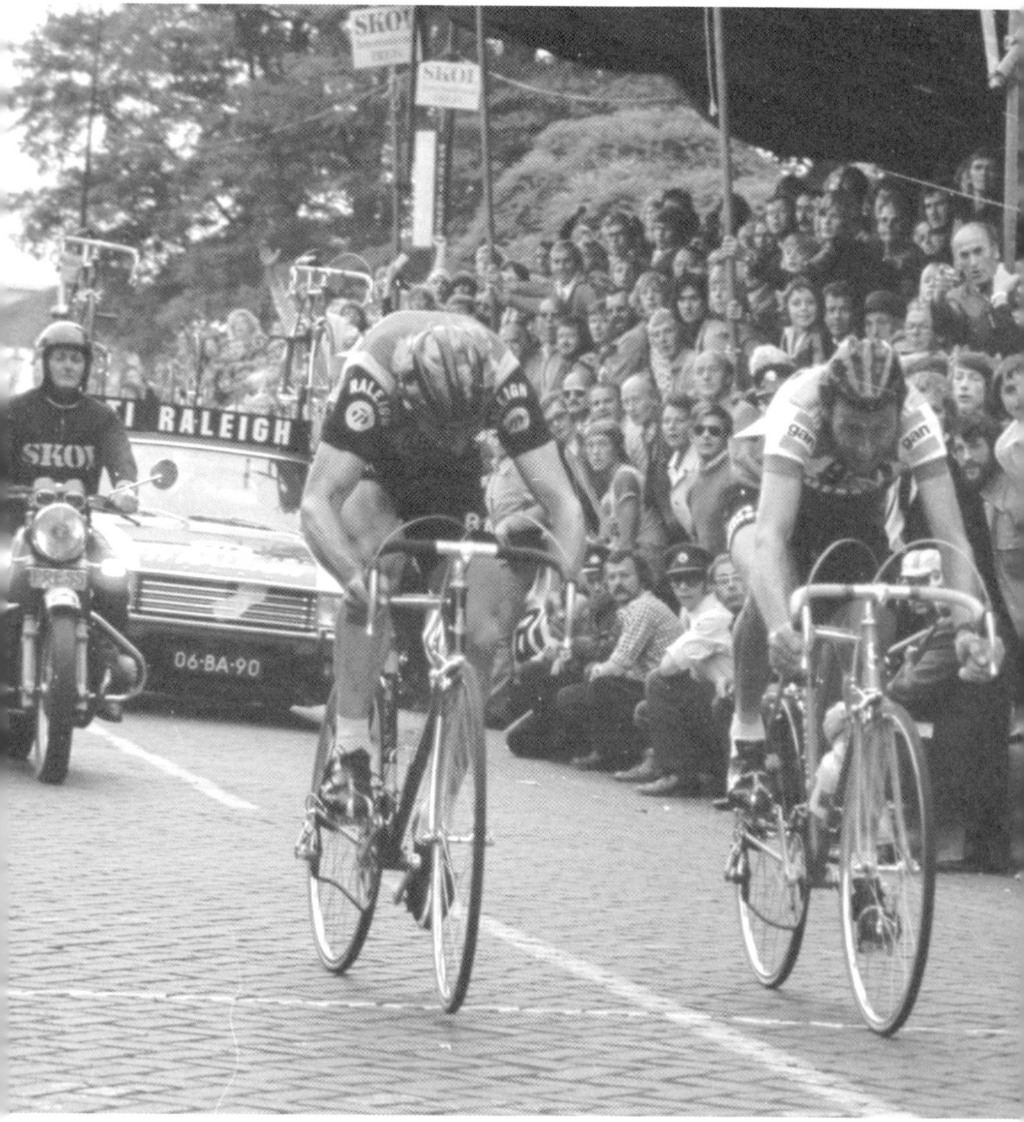
SKOL
SKOL
TI RALEIGH
SKOL
PRESS
06-BA-90
RALEIGH
gan
gan

Who won the 1975 Acht Van Chaam – Tabak, on the left, or Zoetemelk? The finish was so close, Tino didn't know himself.
Netherlands National Library

Tino kept striving for another big win – and sometimes came tantalisingly close. On the 244-kilometre Ghent–Wevelgem classic in Belgium, he attacked on the cobblestones 30 kilometres from the finish – a tried and tested strategy. With a lone lead of almost a minute, Peter Post thought his man was set to win. In the chasing peloton, however, sat the Cannibal, a man renowned for becoming irritable if he went more than a week without a victory.

Merckx got all his men together to chase me down. He wanted to win everything, the arsehole. They caught me [four kilometres from the finish] – 15 of them. Mostly Moltenis [the team] and a passenger, [Englishman] Barry Hoban. He had just been sitting on their wheels. He was a sprinter and he won. Merckx came up afterwards and said, 'Allez, Tino, a disappointment.' Which was a kind of apology.

THE DEAL IN THE DUNES

To vary the training, especially early in the season, Tabak would go for long runs in the sand hills near home. One day he was accompanied by the owner of the local hotel – The White House – who offered him a deal for the future. He could buy the hotel: three storeys, twenty rooms, four billiard tables and two bars. The deal was virtually sealed by the time they got back to town.

When we moved in there was a big 'pub warming' with Peter Post and the Raleigh team, and supporters and radio. I was so popular then. A real celebrity.

My wife worked her heart out, virtually running the place on her own, and raising the kids. But when I returned to the pub after a race everyone wanted to talk to Tino. I was tired, so I started having the occasional drink. It was a disaster waiting to happen, but everyone was telling me it was great.

Even Eddy Merckx acknowledged Tino's disappointment after the Ghent–Wevelgem classic. Yet again, Tabak had proved that in road racing the victor is not always the most deserving.
Adrian Thornton Collection

The worlds of cycling and pub management provided an initially alluring, but ulitmately disastrous, combination. Thirty years later the memories would still be painful. But for now, with everyone's encouragement, Tabak continued riding.

Just as the good cyclists were driven to win, so the managers – especially Peter Post – were driven to see their teams win. Eventually, Tabak tired of being pushed to the limit.

One of the biggest threats to Merckx in 1975 was Belgian road champion Freddy 'The Ogre' Maertens. Tabak and Maertens, with two other riders, made a breakaway in a stage of the Tour of Belgium. Tabak was riding to win, until Maertens offered him a deal. Tabak began working harder at the front to keep the breakaway ahead of the peloton. His efforts were not lost on Peter Post. The manager drove up alongside Tabak and ordered him to stop taking turns. Tabak ignored him and continued riding for the security money Maertens had offered.

Realising that a deal must have been struck, Post threatened to dock Tabak's pay if he did not ride to win. Maertens' response was to offer Raleigh's captain a place on his team. So Tabak kept helping. But when the finish line weaved into sight, instinct took over. Tabak began to sprint. All deals were off. He was drawing alongside the Belgian champion when suddenly a hand clawed at the back of his cycling top. Maertens' teammate! Yanking him back into line.

After the race, Post confronted Tabak. Despite Tabak being able to show a ripped pocket, their relationship soured. Post's autocratic leadership had been effective for a time, but it was bound to breed resentment and rebellion eventually – especially in a 'difficult' individual such as Tabak. Perhaps Post was also sceptical about Tabak's purchase of the White House hotel. Was he a publican or a bike rider? Before long, both his drinks and his cycling were on the rocks.

*They called him
The Cannibal
because he won
everything,
and wanted
everything.
If he turned up
to a race, you'd
think, 'Damn,
I'm riding for
second place.'*

Eddy Merckx gained his gruesome nickname from a 12-year-old girl. Rider Christian Raymond had been telling his daughter about racing with Merckx and she exclaimed, 'That Belgian, he doesn't even leave you the crumbs ... he's a cannibal!'

From one race to the next Merckx wasn't unbeatable. But in his best year he won almost half the races he entered. His impressive tally of victories remains unbeaten.

Lance Armstrong will never be a cycling legend, not compared to Merckx. Lance was a Tour de France legend, not a cycling legend. Merckx won all the tours, classics, criteriums, world road championships and set the hour record. You'll never get another Merckx because riders are specialising so much now. And that's good, because it would be sad to have anyone take that away from him.

A SUNDAY IN HELL

You don't think – you just do. If you think of the risks, you're out the back.

La Pascale, the Queen of the Classics, the Hell of the North. Situated in northern France, the second half of the 260-kilometre Paris–Roubaix is dominated by long stretches of narrow cobblestone roads, so rough and bumpy that, these days, most top riders refuse to enter. In Tabak's years it was mandatory. He raced with the giants: Eddy Merckx, Roger de Vlaeminck and Hennie Kuiper.

The Hell of the North originally referred to the desolate battlefields of the First World War, which the race, described by the 1919 winner as 'a pilgrimage', slowly traversed. The phrase later became synonymous with the cobblestones of the region that were laid down centuries earlier, and are now protected by heritage orders, and maintained especially for bicycle races. Modern bicycles, three kilograms lighter than those of the 1970s, are good for one race only across the cobbles, and then they are retired.

They shake hell out of you. And if it's wet you slip and slide through the mud, with riders crashing left, right and centre. I loved the thrill of it. Paris–Roubaix was an adventure.

Riding through the cobbles in '73, I was in fourth or fifth position. Once again Merckx was up the front. I had a buckled back wheel and told my manager I had to change it. He said, 'No, no – race on!'

A few kilometres later, I asked again, and was refused again. But I was getting pissed off with this buckled wheel, so I just stopped. The car had to skid to stop in time and he actually knocked me over. I got the wheel, but never saw the front four riders again. My manager was so angry. If I'd just unclipped the rear brake and ridden on ... maybe I could have got fifth. Maybe the wheel would have folded under me.

Tabak and many others rode the 260 kilometres to the velodrome in Roubaix with especially wide tyres. Some even used wooden rims to help absorb the shock of the cobblestones. If the weather was bad, crashes and DNFs soon filled up the broom wagon.

One time I was in the broom wagon with lots of other riders. The weather was terrible. Everyone had their own story to tell about pulling out. Hennie Kuiper was still out riding, coming last. I yelled out to him, 'Come on Hennie, get in here.' We were frustrated because we wanted to get into the showers. He was so far behind, but he turned around and said, 'One day I'm going to win this race.' And he kept on riding. He was something special. Not a classy rider, but he had character.

In 1983, on his 11th attempt, Hennie Kuiper won the Paris–Roubaix.

Paris–Roubaix was a race that handicapped team tactics and favoured desperados – like Tabak. But like many Paris–Roubaix protagonists, he was unlucky. He raced four times, against fields of 150 riders, and achieved a best placing of 18th.

DREAMS AND DEMONS

Freddy was good for it. The deal the two riders had made on the road the previous year saw the now 30-year-old Tabak saddle up for the big Flandria-Velda team. Maertens was in phenomenal form, matching Eddy Merckx's best tally of 54 victories in one year. By contrast, Maertens' domestique, Tino Tabak, was starting to struggle. His job was to help Maertens in the first three-quarters of a race, after which the team lieutenants, Michel Pollentier and Marc Demeyer, would take over.

If I'd done all my work well, then no questions were asked. I could hop in the broom wagon for all they cared. But I was never comfortable with that. In my subconscious mind I was peed off.

Tabak raced his fourth and final Tour de France in July 1976. At one point, he was competing for the *Lanterne Rouge* (the Red Lantern, last rider overall). Ironically, this was a coveted role. The tenacious recipient won the hearts of the sporting public, and was guaranteed lucrative contracts in post-Tour criteriums. However, a French rider was being helped towards the same goal. With his manager providing accurate time breaks, the Frenchman calculated exactly how slowly he could go without missing each stage cut-off time. Tabak realised he couldn't win without similar assistance, so he gave it away, and finally, on Stage 15, was disqualified for being pushed too many times by spectators while climbing the Col du Tourmalet. The legal limit was five pushes: an official following Tabak claimed he had lost count.

In his biography, *Fall from Grace*, Maertens, who won eight stages of that Tour, humorously explained: 'You had to make sure you weren't pushed. A course commissioner [followed] in a car, watching you closely ... It was a question, then, of making a clear gesture with your arm behind your back that you didn't want pushing, while at the same time calling "*Poussez! Poussez!*" without being noticed.'

In any case, the ideal number of riders to finish in Paris was decided by the organisers well before the Tour even started. Riders were discreetly disqualified a few at a time until the target had been reached. Naturally, the stragglers were the first to go.

After a rider has passed his peak, he struggles to decide what to do next. Retire? To what? Tabak had given his life to professional cycling. He had no other skills and no other aspirations. So he kept riding.

I was frightened to stop cycling because I didn't have nothing. What was I going to do after cycling? What? Work? We used to laugh at the people we saw working. Workers were idiots and we were heroes. I'd bought the pub, but that wasn't helping. It was a disaster waiting to happen.

In Belgium, races took place virtually every day of the week. Even the small villages would hold a bike race on the day of their annual fair. At every race, almost every day of the year, there were 20 or 30 prizes to be won. The prizes were money, ranging from several hundred dollars for first prize down to $25 for 30th place. It was tempting for riders to race too often and wear themselves down. The chance of winning made it addictive, and had created a sub-culture of 'prize riders'.

I had a yearly contract and got paid once a month. But it wasn't much. The prize money topped it off. You'd pick out a village race, somewhere out of the way, hoping to hell that no one was there so you had a chance of putting a win on your list and earning a little extra. You'd get there, and there'd probably be 150 others that thought the same thing. So it was sort of hit and miss.

The better riders didn't take part in this daily racing, except in their own home towns. The lower riders rode a lot of them, or all of them – prize riders, aiming to get into the first 30. It's a very bad system. You just get up, pack your bags, ride, go home. At home you say, 'I had a prize today.' Then do the same the next day.

Eddy Merckx sometimes started in such races, treating them as training rides and pulling out when he felt like it. But Tabak wasn't getting paid as much as Merckx. Nowhere near it. So he took the village races seriously and raced them far too often.

It was a vicious, criminal world. Before the race you'd see what sort of combine you could get into. That may or may not work. Then you had to wheel and deal with the bookmakers. They were there on the side of the road with their blackboards showing the odds. And if it was arranged that you would win, then you damn well won. You did whatever it took to win.

In one race I lined up next to a swagger with hairy legs, and a bike with a bell and a light on it as if he was going cycle touring. Then the next thing I found I was looking at the arse end of him and struggling to catch up. I thought, this can't be happening to me! But of course, he was in a combine, and had jumped. If you took off after him, there would be someone on your wheel. You soon learn.

Apart from combines, supporters and bookmakers, the riders also had drug testing officials to consider. In the big races, the top three place-getters and one or two random riders would be tested.

The village races weren't often tested, but if they were, it might be with little or no warning.

In one criterium Tabak was passed a bidon near the finish. It felt empty. Inside a note read simply 'B.O.B.' – the Belgian Drug Brigade. The B.O.B. meant business. They might be acting on a tip-off, or they might have searched the changing rooms, or it could just be a routine process. The testing squad would form a 'V' around the finishing line, and anyone who crossed it could be taken away. Before the finish, Tabak veered off the course, headed straight to his car and drove home – and those long drives home could be terrible.

I was going to Belgium almost every day, taking pills and not giving myself time to rest. I could feel good, but then as it wears off, you get back to reality. I had ups and downs – and I mean really down. I felt the changes in my body while driving home after a race. I had nothing other than cycling. I was living in my own world.

I had a good wife, and I didn't realise it because everything revolved around me. I would start training at 9am, and be home at 5pm, and my bath would be ready, and I mean ready. On the stool beside the bath were my clothes, ironed. Then everyone had to be quiet because Tino was tired. Everyone was walking around on tiptoes because of me. This started when I was riding well, and carried on when I wasn't riding well, just being a fuckwit to myself and still getting the same treatment from her.

But Tino Tabak wasn't just tired. He was deeply unhappy in his sport, which had become a business for him, and each night he returned home struggling to recover, as much as possible, from the medication he was taking. Riders were mostly using straight amphetamines and sleeping pills, although anabolic steroids were also common – used to mitigate the wasting of muscle from racing too often. Tabak was apprehensive of steroids, and resorted to them only in his last few years. At his most desperate, though, he tried doubling the dose.

I boosted the preparation to 50ml and started training at the same time because I thought I would have a better season. After a month, I got all confused and scared. I felt as if I was becoming a woman; started growing breasts. I didn't feel healthy at all. I took a risk and it didn't pay off.

It took decades for the medical profession to widely release information on the medium- to long-term negative effects of amphetamines. The German army had relied heavily on amphetamine use during the Blitzkrieg of the Second World War and knew within a few years that the drug had undesirable secondary effects, associated with dependence. Records documented depression,

For Tabak's last few years as a professional, all the riders and events just merged into one.
Adrian Thornton Collection

psychosis and paranoia – sometimes serious. One record tells of a German patrol firing all its ammunition at imaginary Russians and then nervously surrendering. The British and US forces also used truckloads of amphetamines, with British Field Marshal Montgomery ordering the supply of 100,000 tablets for the initial assault in the battle of El Alamein.

After the war, military scientists warned of 'impaired judgment', stating that the amphetamine user 'feels that he is doing well, when in fact he is making all sorts of mistakes'. By the 1970s, the negative effects were confirmed and amphetamines were greatly restricted. Studies showed that 15–20 per cent of amphetamine users became dependent, and there was no way of knowing who would develop compulsive habits.

Habitual users, and by 1976 there were hundreds of thousands, commonly developed symptoms of irritability, sleeplessness and anxiety. With continued use, this often led to amphetamine psychosis whereby paranoid delusions led users to do irrational things.

Amphetamine at the races, and alcohol back at the hotel at night, transported Tabak away from the grinding reality of professional cycling – but only temporarily. At first it made anything seem possible, but now nothing seemed possible without it.

Amphetamine is like alcohol. You start off drinking a couple of stubbies, and you're happy and drunk, then after a while you get used to it and have to drink a whole bloody crate, and you're still not happy and still not drunk.

I thought I had pretty good control of myself. But when the problems of racing and running the hotel started, I got past a certain point, and I just needed to escape. It was all false – totally false. But you don't realise till later. You sort of lose yourself. I lost Tino – he was gone.

Of course the outside world could see the problem. It was affecting my family life, my social life, everything. I knew it was a downhill journey, but for some crazy reason, I was still in a sort of fantasy world, thinking I could win races. Even though reality was showing it was no good, I wouldn't give in.

Few cycling teams had qualified doctors who could monitor the effects on individuals or administer safe doses. It was a *fabrieksgeheim* – a trade secret kept behind closed doors. Other riders and soigneurs offered advice, especially to top competitors, but as a rider's performances dropped and the imperative to improve increased, advice and support usually dwindled.

In the beginning, I was a New Zealander, and everyone was interested in me, but as time went on I became one of the general riders – some people support you, some don't.

I remember missing a break once and trying to get back up to the front bunch and having spectators booing, and telling me I couldn't do it any more and my time was over. It's the normal criticism you get if people aren't your supporters. In Belgium and France, they end up fighting each other. Supporters can be nasty and put so much pressure on that the riders end up quitting or going to a nut house – or taking illegal drugs. On the way to a race you might think, 'I'm not feeling too good today,' but they'd paid 25 guilders or whatever to see you. We're talking about hundreds of people, sometimes thousands. You always had to perform.

The supporters groups would be in the [event] cafe before the race, and when we went to sign in they would say, 'Hey, Tino. How's it going? Are you going to win today?' Little did they know that I had already made a combina and another rider was arranged to win, not me!

But if the race is in my village then I win. It's arranged [by the combina] and I ride to win, but I might come second because another combine is trying to win as well.

People in your village would put money up for primes and expect you to win them. You'd start psyching yourself up in the morning.

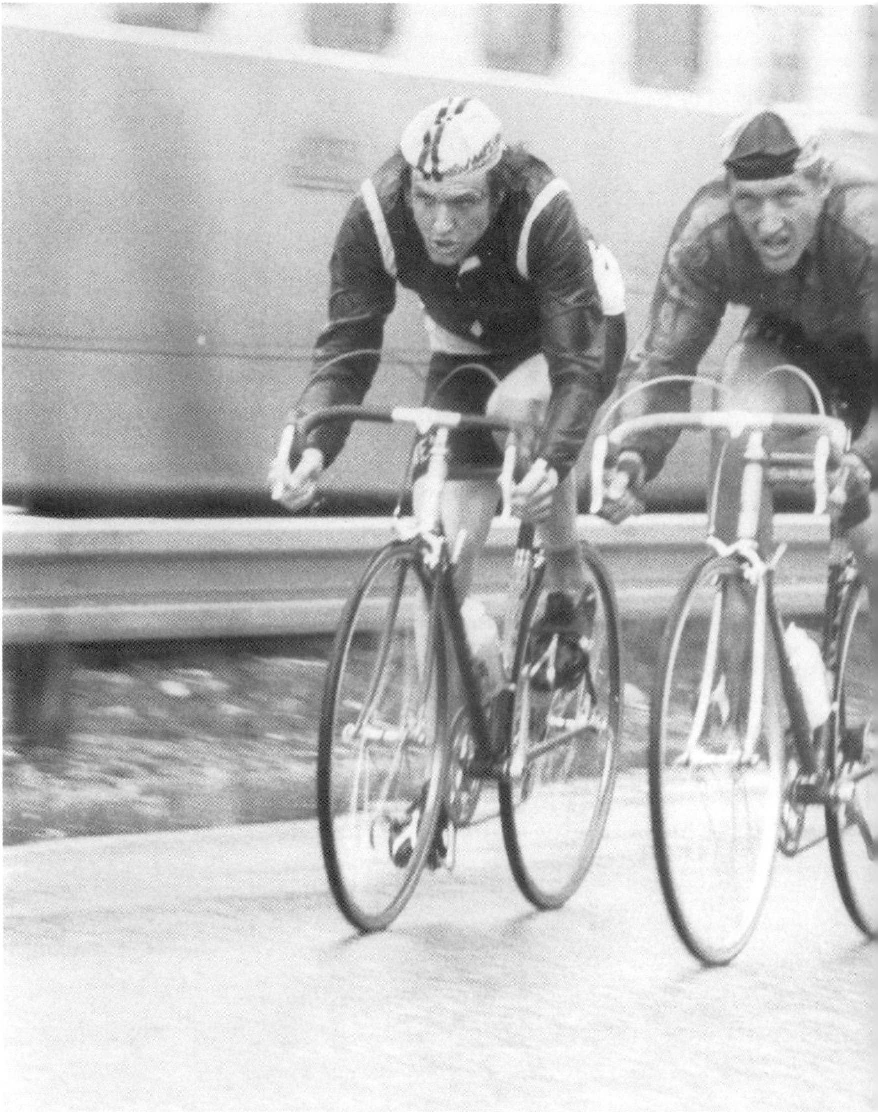

Another breakaway in the rain.
The Tabak Collection

Go for a pre-race warm-up and everyone would be saying, 'Hope you win tonight, Tino', and it preys on your mind. Then I plan it out, organise a combine to win and give it everything.

Like all celebrities, Tabak was constantly meeting obsessive supporters who adored him for his success – both men and women. *I was like a sailor with a girl in every port.* Life was becoming very, very complicated.

When we came home from Belgium one night I went into a cafe on the border for a cup of coffee, and there was a guy at the bar who asked what we'd been doing. We said we'd been at the race, and he said, 'Oh yeah, I usually always go.' So I asked, 'Who do you support?' and he replied, 'Tino Tabak.' 'Do you?!' 'Yeah, I usually help him with his bike and washing gear.' We laughed and just thought he was a crazy supporter. He was telling Tino all about Tino.

And as is the case in any sport, when he was winning, fans shared in his success by glorifying him. But when he wasn't winning, the barflies back at the White House were quick to offer advice and criticism. After a hard day's racing, that was the last thing he needed. Inevitably, tempers flared.

The pressures that had been building for years finally boiled over. The first thing to go was the White House. (*It should have been called Devil's Kingdom.*) One or two social drinks had developed into a serious problem. Desperate to escape, Tabak stuffed all the accounts into a plastic bag and stormed out. He dumped them on his accountant's desk and shouted, *That's it. Finished.*

His wife was furious that he could abandon the hotel; after all her hard work, just walk out without warning. But the drinking culture made him feel like he was on death row.

Alcohol is the worst drug of the lot. More families and sportspeople are ruined by it than anything.

Tino and Mieke, along with children Paul and Melanie, moved south and stayed in a caravan beside the harbour at Rotterdam for the next year. He was running low on friends – no drinks, no drinking buddies – but the big jovial restaurateur Joop Zijlaard recognised Tabak's problems and watched out for him. Not only did he supply the caravan but soon Zijlaard was helping Tabak to train for the Bordeaux–Paris.

THE LAST BIG RACE

The Bordeaux–Paris of 1977 was the last big race in which Tabak would place highly – and he couldn't have picked a bigger one. This venerable classic, first run in 1891, was the longest one-day race in Europe. Its 560-kilometre course was divided in two: the first half was unpaced, with riders jostling in a bunch as usual. Then after a 20-minute break, they headed off individually behind Dernys (motorised bicycles with no gears – a unique model had been made for the event and appropriately named the Bordeaux–Paris).

Tabak was by now in a B-grade team, sponsored by Dutch oil company De Onderneming. The team lacked glamour or power. Bordeaux–Paris seemed like a good choice of race – as the longest one-day race in Europe it presented hours of opportunity to lesser riders. Tabak was determined to make the most of this opportunity.

There were strict doping controls, but I had this special thing to inject at the halfway break. In the first half, I was feeling pretty good, and we got into Poitiers where the transition was. I went to the toilets; they were squat-down ones with saloon-type doors. I was sort of looking over the top, to see if anyone was coming. The needle was huge and I couldn't get it in, and my bum was bleeding. I didn't even know what this stuff was. I'd got it from a friend of a friend who said it was 'bloody good stuff', and it was legal, supposedly. I got half of it in and flushed the rest down the toilet.

Then my soigneur gave me sports drink and told me to drink lots.

In the second half, we had to stop to fill the Derny's tank, and my pacemaker, Joop, told me we were going to attack. I said, 'All right.' So we attacked, and I felt shit hot and got a few minutes on the field. There was radio, TV, motorbikes — it's an exciting kick. That's the whole buzz of cycling. I felt so strong, until after another couple of hours. Then I felt real bad. My legs were absolutely stuffed. So the pacer said to put my little finger in the back hole of the Derny seat and get towed along.

We did this for as long as no one was around to see. And when officials came by and stayed too long I was in serious pain cycling. In the last couple of kilometres, though, I brightened up and focused on the finish.

In Tabak's last great success the riders were paced behind Dernys such as these.
Les Woodland Collection

Tabak placed seventh in the Bordeaux–Paris, an impressive result for a rider in a budget team. His sponsors were ecstatic. But Tabak knew he was hitting the bottom of the barrel.

I had no pride. I wasn't important any more. Deep down it started eating at me. The world that I lived in – I was mentally not right for – never. I was right for New Zealand but not the European scene. At first I absolutely loved it. Then I got to a stage when I absolutely detested it, and that happened very quickly. I was unable to motivate myself without taking something. I didn't tell my family. I should have ... should have played open cards and then I might have got myself into a different situation.

Was Tino not right for the world of professional racing, or was the world of professional racing not right for him? The physical and psychological demands were so great that casualties were inevitable. It was all too much: too many races; too many supporters; too much at stake. Depression, drug dependence and death were all too common among riders of the 1960s and 1970s.

In the middle of the 1977 season Tabak's friend and former Raleigh teammate, Bas Hordijk, died during a criterium. He'd been invited for dinner that very night, but as Tabak phrases it, 'his heart stopped'. Later in the year it was the turn of Wim Prinsen, a former Goudsmit-Hoff teammate, whom Tabak used to pick up on the way to races in Belgium; his heart stopped. A few years later, former Flandria teammate Marc Demeyer, while doing the crossword at home; his heart stopped. Some, like Erik de Vlaeminck, checked themselves into psychiatric care before it was too late and recovered. Luis Ocaña battled on within himself for years before finally putting a gun to his head.

In the last year [1978], the money was terrible and I was just surviving. I was in a small 12-man team sponsored by Zoppa-Zeus, Italian criminals I think. I only met the owner once at a crazy birthday party for a 100-year-old parrot. He had two bodyguards — the owner, not the parrot. He came in, met us, and left. I never saw him again.

Zoppa-Zeus was a Z-grade team. The rubbish team. I just made up the field. At the next race, you'd always hope you'd come right again, but I was doing totally the wrong things for that to happen. I needed pills to race, pills to sleep and pills to wake up. I was gambling it all, and not even realising it until it was too late.

A toxic combination of stress, fatigue, pills and depression led the fallen star to question the value of his own existence. Fighting demons every day. Hardly surviving. Despising himself. When it was finally all too much, he walked out ... not fully conscious of where he was going ... looking for a final solution. From the edge of a high bridge, he gazed out across the abyss. It was beautiful: the space, the flowing water, the solitude. Too beautiful. He stood there a long, long time, until he became part of it. Everything and nothing. Then stepped back.

During my down period, I left home and hid in the cellar of Jan Haile, a soigneur who became a personal friend. I was going through a real bad patch, when everything started going wrong. He helped me ... or didn't. Another friend found me and told me to go home. But I didn't go, not at first. I was frightened. Everything was tumbling down, physically and mentally. Lots of bad decisions I made and good decisions I didn't make. After hiding, I tried to cut back to half the bad stuff. It doesn't work. I needed to get out of it completely — out of the jungle. I was mentally empty. Just totally empty.

Tino Tabak had been racing fulltime since leaving the railways in 1966. Five successful years as an amateur had preceded almost eight years and more than 1,000 races as a professional. Setting off on the 1978 Tour of Holland, he tightened his toe-straps for the last professional race of his career. It was a wet, miserable day that the riders pushed off into for the second stage. As the bunch flew around a sharp corner, Tabak's front wheel hit the wheel in front of him and he slid out. At 40 kilometres per hour, his thigh, shoulder and head hit the road. His head was split open.

Straight away I knew it was finished. I didn't shed a tear. It was over.

This time, there was no manager to put him back on his bike. No sympathetic supporters eager to help. Suffering from concussion, he was taken to hospital in Apeldoorn. He never returned to professional racing.

FINDING TINO

Every sportsperson knows what it's like to lose. To lose the dream. But the reality of losing seems like a dream itself – until you lose everything.

By the age of 32, Tino Tabak had ridden out of himself into a bleak no man's land. Youthful dreams and ambitions had become obscured and meaningless. Though his injuries from the fall in the Tour of Holland needed only a few days in hospital, the break enabled Tabak to see beyond the fog of bicycle racing – revealing a stark reality. What he once lived for was now killing him.

On one level, Tabak had understood the problems for some time, but it was in hospital that he finally made the resolution to quit. His wife – relieved beyond expression – immediately helped him to look for work outside cycling.

He was admitted to hospital on Wednesday. Discharged on Saturday. Went down to the wharves at Ijmuiden on Monday. Life changed so quickly. Tabak found a fishing manager – a friend of a friend of a friend. After brief introductions, the boss said, 'Righto. Go on to that ship. Jan will show you what to do.'

I'd never been on a fishing boat before, but I looked around and found Jan down in the hatch. He showed me how to stack fish and unload boats. It had to be done fast, and was hard work. I quite enjoyed it.

At the end of the day, the boss said, 'Okay, I see you in the morning.'

On the way home, Tabak stopped in town and bought the same sort of denim clothes the fishermen wore and the same type of tobacco they smoked. The next morning at 5am, he was back, unloading fishing boats; it was the start of 14 to 15 hours' work a day for the next five years. He worked with a strong crew, mostly gypsies who didn't know who he was and took him on face value. Everyone was on the same level.

It was a good period. I only had to worry about work. It made me realise how unimportant I had become as a cyclist. I loved being part of a crew, doing work that really mattered. Working with big, solid, healthy, worn-out men. The tasks were obvious and there was a very ordered and simple social structure. Just work, no hierarchy crap, no deals or double-crossing. Just one boss – and he cracked the whip.

On the wharves there was no time for pills. I wasn't completely cured, but mostly over it. You're never completely cured. There is always some time, or time of year, when I'm craving, and have to make a choice. That will always be with me. You can't take away memories. They won't go. But the willpower to say no, you can create that.

Over the next ten years, Tabak moved between jobs: crewing on fishing boats, working on oil rigs, setting up scaffolding on building sites. His family life improved. Then he was drawn back to sport, competing in marathons and triathlons, training cyclists and running a trophy shop. He was approached to promote a sports drink, and put an enormous effort into the challenge for two years.

But I didn't have the financial strength or legal rights to carry it. I mixed the recipe, got it canned, took it to events.

But the pressures of competing once more, this time to sell the drink, and juggling work commitments with sporting events and family life began to take hold and finally Mieke could take no more. *I lost both my family and the sports drink. I don't blame her. She left me and it was the best decision she could make. Everything revolved around me — it was a selfishness I'd created around myself as a kid and reinforced with cycle racing. I should never have got married. I wasn't right for it until I was about 50. No thought for other people. Didn't appreciate a lot of what was done for me. It took a long time for me to realise how I was living. It was all an ego-inflated fantasy balloon, just waiting to pop.*

It catches up with you in the finish. I was tired of life. It's not something that medication or counselling can help you with. You need to sit down and have a good talk with yourself and try to find yourself. Look for Tino — 'Hello, where are you?' I was in my late forties when I tried to find Tino — he kept on running away. And then you catch him, come to terms and make an agreement. If you can make an agreement with yourself and start saying and thinking good things about yourself, then you're starting to go in the right direction.

With his family, his business and most of his friends gone, Tabak continued his association with cycling by training Monica Valvik of Norway. Their goal was the 1994 women's world road championships in Italy. He was a tough trainer, but she was equally tough and after several months' training she won the world title in a sprint finish. With the title came fame and fortune. Everyone was drawn to the Valvik light, everyone but Tabak.

Three months after the championships he drove across Norway to Oslo Airport. No cyclists were there to see him off, and there would be none to greet him when he landed. The final boarding call came, and Tino Tabak climbed slowly up the aluminium staircase and in to a plane bound for the other side of the world. Twenty-seven years in the Netherlands, and he still didn't feel Dutch. The plane taxied up the runway. Twenty-seven years. It lifted off. Half his life. And sketched a jet-trail across the northern sky.

After two days' travel Tino touched down in Christchurch and remembered something his father had said a long time ago.

I'm a Kiwi now.

EPILOGUE

October 18, 2002. A small cluster of farmhouses nestles beside a narrow canal on the Canterbury Plains. The nor'wester harries strips of high wispy cloud, and Mt Hutt in the distance anchors the fields to the horizon.

For some time I've been asking around for 'Tino Tabak, the racing cyclist? ... He did the Tour de France. In the 1970s ... ?'

A tramping friend of mine saw him painting houses in Methven, but now he works at the freezing works. None of the locals seem to have heard of him. Perhaps he likes it that way. I leave my number just in case. Eventually, when I've about given up, the phone rings and barks, *You're talking to Tino Tabak!* The following week, I'm travelling down to the plains for an interview.

It's so quiet. If he has neighbours they must be monks. Not a sound can be heard apart from the occasional baaing sheep and the quardling of one or two magpies.

After untangling the wires on the tape recorder, I push play for the first of many times over several years, and a story starts to unfold. It's a sad and joyful, complicated yet simple story of strength and weakness, victories and downfalls, and a multitude of contradictions. Mr Tabak is intense and forthright.

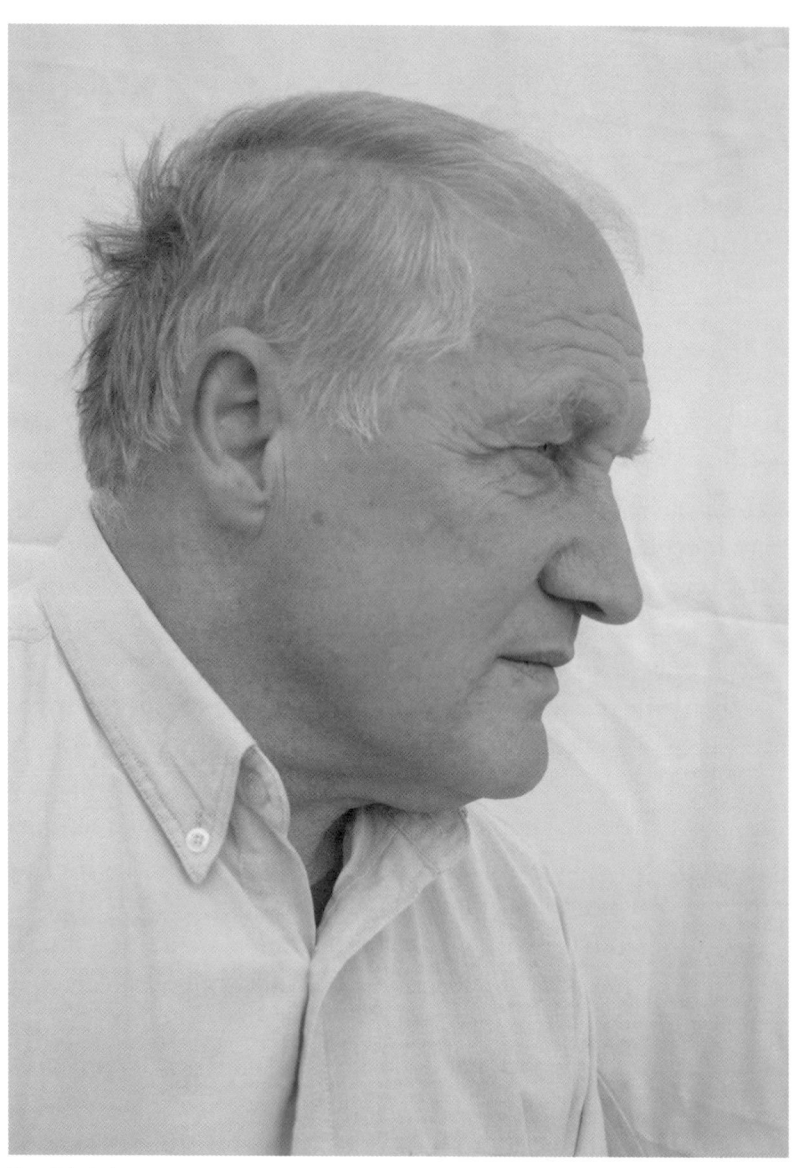

Tino Tabak, 2008   *Jonathan Kennett*

When I was racing and winning, I had so many friends – or people who I thought were my friends. But when it comes down to the nitty-gritty, when you've got nothing any more, then you find you've got no one. Zilch. Not a soul. Where do they all go?

That's why I like living out here. The people who put the effort into coming to see me are real friends. I always said I would come back to New Zealand. It's my home. Deep in my subconscious I'm Dutch, but this is my home, and it's the best place in the world. People don't realise how good we have it here. I've got a good partner, a good job and a good garden.

The stunning garden wraps itself around a modest home, framing it with a kaleidoscope of bright colours. In the paddock out back, fifty free-range chickens and two plump sheep help keep Tino busy. A friendly old dog totters around, trying to keep up. Jess was his last training companion, and when she grew too old to run beside him, Tino hung up his bike.

If I look back, and ask, 'Was it worth it?' – of course it was. I've lapped it out with the Cannibal in the Tour de France, and I've struggled just for the dubious Red Lantern. I've beaten Holland's best to claim their road championship title, and I've risked everything to win a classic, almost following Tommy Simpson's fate. It was madness. I can see that now. But people sometimes still say, 'Tino Tabak the bike rider? Yeah, he was all right.' And I think to myself, 'He was fuckin good, really.' I was good. I can honestly say that now. But I should have been better. A lot better. End of story!

WHERE ARE THEY NOW?

Hennie Kuiper: Raced with steady success through to his retirement in 1988, aged 39. After racing he became a team manager and now he works for the Rabobank team in public relations.

Freddy Maertens: Nicknamed the Ogre, Freddy had a wildly erratic career marked by phenomenal success and psychological difficulties. After retiring from racing in 1987 he lost most of his money through bad business deals and was pursued by the tax authorities. He now works at the Tour of Flanders museum in Belgium.

Eddy Merckx: The Cannibal won 525 professional races, more than any other rider in history, and is still considered the greatest rider of all time. After cycling he ran a bicycle factory and in 2004 he took up recreational cycling.

Jesus Luis Ocaña: Finally won the Tour de France in 1973, but because Eddy Merckx wasn't there he was considered a *faux* winner. In 1977 he retired from cycling and thereafter he struggled to run his vineyard. He was dogged by unsuccessful business deals, depression and ill health. In 1994 he shot himself.

Peter Post: Retired in 1995, ranked as the second most successful team manager in history (the most successful was Guillaume Driessens, manager for Eddy Merckx). Some claim that several of the riders he managed died young or had personal problems in their lives.

Marinus 'Rini' Wagtmans: In 1972 he retired early from cycle racing because of heart problems. Eventually he became a successful businessman.

Joop Zoetemelk: During his 18 years as a professional bike racer Zoetemelk started and finished 16 Tours de France, more than any other rider. In 1985, at the age of 38, he became the oldest rider ever to win the world road cycling championships. He was a cycling official for ten years and then ran a hotel near Paris, which he recently retired from.

Christchurch co-markers: John Cleary died of cancer in 2007. He continued riding until the 1980s. Ross Bush, Roger Fowler and Graeme Milner are all retired, but still regularly cycle long distances, and each still recalls, 'I actually beat Tino once. Of course, he was a junior then.'

KEY RACE RESULTS
Major events are marked in bold

AMATEUR

1963 By the end of 1963, the 17-year-old Tabak had ridden in 82 races, won 10 and gained 47 fastest times
6th against the seniors, Timaru to Christchurch (100 miles)

1964 6th **Tour of Southland**
Fastest time, Christchurch–Akaroa–Christchurch (2 stages, 104 miles, 4h 24m 30s)
Fastest time, Canterbury Round the Gorges Classic (100 miles – 4h 8m 3s)

1965 1st team, New Zealand Junior 4000m Team Pursuit with G Sword, J Cleary and M Litolff
Fastest time and new record, Hokitika to Greymouth (25 miles)
Fastest time (record), Avon 4-mile Hill Climb (14m 29s)
1st and fastest time, Christchurch Around the Bays (40 miles)
Fastest time, Christchurch Around the Harbour (40 miles)
Fastest time, Timaru Alan Roach Memorial Open (50 miles)
1st, Avon–Glenmore 25-mile criterium
Fastest junior time, Buller 100-mile Open
Fastest time, Marlborough 50-mile Championship
Fastest time, Shirley Lodge Classic (80 miles)
Fastest time, Christchurch–Akaroa–Christchurch
2nd fastest time (by a wheel), Timaru to Christchurch (100 miles)
Fastest time, Round the Gorges (100 miles in record time of 4h 1m 21s)
1st, **Tour of Southland** (15h 26m 54s) and 1st equal, KOM
2nd, Canterbury Road Championship (100 miles)
1st Senior 100-mile **National Road Championships**, Dunedin

1966 Breaks Australasian hour record (42.91km) at English Park, Christchurch
1st, 4000m Pursuit at Caledonian Society's sports meeting in Timaru
1st **New Zealand 4000m Track Championship** (5m 14.5s)
1st team, 4000m Team Pursuit with J Cleary, R Mann and P Skilling
3rd, second Commonwealth Games Trial (Morrinsville, 120 miles)
Fastest time, Christchurch Frank Grose Memorial (50 miles)
1st and fastest time, Christchurch Around the Bays (40 miles)
Fastest time and new record, Christchurch Around the Harbour (42 miles)
1st and fastest time, Masterton Open (54 miles)
Fastest time (record) and second place, Shirley Lodge Classic (80 miles)

3rd, **National Road Championships** in Taradale (100 miles)
1st, **Tour of Manawatu**, by 17 seconds (8h 34m 10s)
1st, **Tour of Southland**, by 10 seconds (14h 16m 46s)
1st, **Dulux Six Day Cycle Race**, by 2 minutes (26h 43m 55s)
Tabak crowned Canterbury Sportsman of the Year

1967 Fastest time and record time, Buller 100-mile Open
1st, final Air New Zealand Cycling Grand Prix at Palmerston North (2 days, 222 miles)
1st, 80-mile Hobart Handicap Road Race
Fastest time, Christchurch–Akaroa–Christchurch (2 stages, 104 miles)
3rd fastest time, 100-mile Taranaki Round the Mountain Classic (sprinted on the line. Fastest time went to Bryce Beeston, a race record of 3h 46m 54s)
1st, **Tour of Manawatu**, by over 1 minute (250 miles, 8h 34m 46s)
1st, **Dulux Six Day Cycle Race**, by 4 minutes (28h 27m 45s)
1st, **Tour of Southland**, by 4½ minutes (14h 9m 44s), 1st equal KOM
Breaks his own one-hour Australasian record at English Park (43.44km)

1968 Wins the first in a series of club races in Amsterdam
1st, Venhuizen 100km criterium (NED)
2nd, Ghent–Ieper 170km classic (BEL)

1969 1st, Venhuizen 100km criterium (NED)
1st, Rynland–Palts (biggest amateur tour in Germany)
2nd, Tour of Twente (150km) (note: John Dean 3rd)
3rd, Spectacle of Steenwijk
17th, GC of Olympia's Tour, 7 days in the Netherlands

1970 3rd, **Amateur World Cycling Championships** at Leicester, Britain, as part of Dutch 100km team
1st, **Tour of North Holland** (one-day classic)
1st, Grand Prix of Belgium
7th, **Tour of Britain** (Milk Race) 14 days, 2,160km; 2nd, Stage 3 by a centimetre
10th Olympia's Tour

PROFESSIONAL

1971 Riding for Team Mars-Flandria
Tour de France
Prologue – 3rd, team time trial
Stage 1 – 32nd
Stage 1b – 8th
Stage 1c – 22nd
Stage 2 – 6th (5th in GC)
Stage 3 – 37th (5th in GC)
Stage 4 – 28th (5th in GC)
Stage 5 – 35th (6th in GC)
Stage 6 – 17th (7th in GC)
Stage 6b – 71st (8th in GC)
Stage 7 – 92nd (8th in GC)
Stage 8 – 126th
Stage 9 – 89th (pulls out)
2nd, Melsele
3rd, Tour of Haspengouw (Hannuit)
3rd, Borgehout
3rd, Hansweert
21st, **Tour of Andalucia** (Spain)
45th, **Amstel Gold Race** (Dutch classic: 238km)
48th, **Gent–Wevelgem** (Belgian classic: 237km)

1972 Riding for Team Goudsmit-Hoff
1st, **Netherlands Professional Road Cycling Championships**
1st, Acht van Chaam (100km criterium)
1st, Circuit Des Ardennes Flamandes
3rd, Tour de Levant
3rd, St Willebrord
14th, **Tour of Andalucia** (Spain – 792km) Goudsmit-Hoff was 2nd team
18th, **Tour de France** – 3,846.6km
19th, **Tour of Switzerland** (8 stages and prologue: 1,457km)
21st, **Ghent–Wevelgem** (Belgian classic: 237km)

1973 Riding for Team Sonolor TV
1st, Grand Prix of Cannes
1st, Grand Prix of Menton
1st, 40-lap invitation race (Palmerston North, New Zealand)
2nd, Grand Prix de La Crau
2nd, Evergem
3rd, Kuurne–Brussels–Kuurne (NED)

7th, **Netherlands Professional Road Cycling Championships**
7th, **Tour of Holland**
27th, **Paris–Roubaix** (French 'monument' classic: 272km)
Tour de France
  Stage 1a – 13th
  Stage 2a – 8th, team time trial (10th GC)
  Stage 7a – 14th
  Stage 8 – 107th (last – terrible crash)

1974 Riding for Team TI Raleigh
1st, Circuit of Waasland
1st, Circuit of Kemzeke (Belgium)
1st, Tour of Midden-Zeeland
1st, Grand Prix of Nottingham
1st, Grave (Dutch criterium)
1st, Sas Van Gent (criterium)
1st, Tarleton (met Rene Pijoen)
1st, Uithuizen (criterium)
Awarded Telesport Trophy (most points in Frisol series)
2nd, Circuit of Grensstreek (Ledegem)
2nd, Grand Prix Blackpool
2nd, Grand Prix Morecambe
3rd, Grand Prix Emile Mercier (Nice)
3rd, Tour of South Holland
3rd, Grand Prix Cannes
3rd, Sittard
3rd, Vlijmen
4th, **Tour of Belgium** (5 stages and prologue: 927.7km)
8th, **Amstel Gold Race** (Dutch classic: 238km – 137 riders)
14th, **World Road Championship** at Montreal
16th, **Ghent–Wevelgem** (Belgian classic: 237km)
18th, **Tour of Flanders**
19th, **Tour of Switzerland** (9 stages and prologue: 1,641.6km)

1975 Riding for Team TI-Raleigh
1st, Acht van Chaam (Dutch criterium: 100km)
1st, Wateringen Wielerdag (NED)
2nd, Kuurne–Brussels–Kuurne (NED)
2nd, Dwars door Belgie (Waregem, BEL)
2nd, Grand Prix Maurice Raes (Heusden)
2nd, Petegem/Leie (BEL)
2nd, Stabroek (BEL)
7th, **Tour of Netherlands** (5 stages and prologue: 995.2km)

11th, **Ghent–Wevelgem** (Belgian classic: 237km)
15th, **Tour of Belgium** (5 stages and prologue: 969km)
18th, **Tour of Switzerland** (10 stages and prologue: 1,636.1km)
18th, **Paris–Roubaix** (French 'Monument' classic: 277.5km)

1976 Riding for Team Flandria-Velda
1st, Santpoort (NED)
4th, **Tour of Andalucia** (Ruta del Sol: 7 stages and prologue: 892km), 2nd, first stage; 2nd, mountains, Flandria 2nd team
22nd, **Tour of Switzerland** (9 stages and prologue: 1,466.5km)
72nd, **Milan–San Remo** (288km)
Tour de France
  Prologue – 71st, individual time trial
  Stage 5a – 2nd, team time trial
  Stage 15 – disqualified for being pushed too many times

1977 Riding for Team De Onderneming-Benco-Mavic
7th, **Bordeaux–Paris** (French classic: 597km)
14th, **Tour of Luxembourg** (4 stages: 598km)
45th, **Amstel Gold Race** (Dutch classic: 238km)

1978 Riding for Team Zoppas-Zeus
2nd, Galder
3rd, Arma di Taggia (ITL)
Retires from cycling after crashing in Tour of Holland

I was never happy with seconds or thirds, and I got a lot of them.

NEW ZEALANDERS IN THE TOUR DE FRANCE
General Classification, and top-ten stage placings

Name	Year		Place
Harry Watson	1928		28
		Stage 3	7
		Stage 8	10
Tino Tabak	1971		DNF
		Prologue: team time trial	3
		Stage 1b	8
		Stage 2	6
	1972		18
		Stage 3b: team time trial	7
	1973		DNF
		Stage 2a: team time trial	8
	1976		DNF
		Stage 5a: team time trial	2
Paul Jesson	1979		DNF
Eric MacKenzie	1982		87
		Stage 10	5
		Stage 18	5
		Stage 21	7
	1983		104
		Stage 4	3
		Stage 7	10
		Stage 8	4
	1985		127
		Stage 1	8
		Stage 2	9
		Stage 6	7
		Stage 9	8
		Stage 19	7
		Stage 22	8
	1986		DNF
Nathan Dahlberg	1988		144
	1989		DNF
Stephen Swart	1987		DNF
	1994		112
	1995		109
Chris Jenner	2001		139
		team time trial	1
Julian Dean	2004		127
		Stage 6	8
	2006		128
	2007		107
	2008		110
		Stage 14	4
		Stage 21	6
	2009		121
Hayden Roulston	2009		79

GLOSSARY

Amphetamine (speed, pep pills, confidence pills and uppers): A type of drug commonly used for weight loss, depression, as sport and war performance enhancers, and recreationally.

Attack: To try to outride the following riders, thus forcing them to accelerate and hopefully exhaust themselves trying to keep up.

Bidon (French): A cyclist's drinking bottle.

Broom wagon: A vehicle that follows a race to 'sweep up' or collect the riders who cannot finish.

Cash club: For most of the 20th century there were two types of cycling clubs in New Zealand – the cashies and the amateurs. The cash clubs (later called professional clubs) allowed their riders to accept prize money.

Classic: A prestigious one-day race, often from one town to another, or in one long loop.

Combine: An informal and sometimes secretive group of riders supporting a chosen 'team leader' to win. Any prize money is shared among the combine members (i.e. they are 'in the chop'). A **combina** is the deal such a combine makes.

Criterium (criterion): A race of many laps around a short course. The length of the race can be determined either by the number of laps or by the most laps completed within a set time.

Domestiques (French): Literally 'helpers', a terms used for riders contracted to assist their team leader. Also known as 'servants' and 'water carriers'.

General Classification (GC): The overall time placing for a rider in a tour.

King of the Mountains (KOM): Title given to the best climber of a tour. Points are awarded to the riders first over the top, and climbs are categorised according to steepness and length.

Peloton: The main group of cyclists in a road race.

Prologue: A short race the day before the first stage of a tour, which is part of the tour and can be used to decide the starting order of the riders.

Scratch riders (back markers): The fastest riders in a handicap race start last or 'from scratch'. These riders are expected to catch up to the rest of the field.

Soigneur (French): Assistant responsible for feeding, clothing, massaging and escorting the riders. Some also took on the role of team 'doctor' and supplied riders with performance-enhancing medication.

Yellow jersey (maillot jaune): The jersey worn by the leader in general classification in a multi-stage race.

SOURCES

Quotes from Tino Tabak are shown in italics throughout the book. Almost all quotes have come from interviews with the author and some of these have been edited. A small number are quotes from newspapers.

Books

Fotheringham, William. *A Century of Cycling: The Classic Races and Legendary Champions*. London: Mitchell Beazley, 2003.

Kane, Karl. *C'est une Grande Fete: The Tour de France and Experiential Design Theory* (Phd. Thesis). Wellington: Massey University, 2007.

Kennett Brothers, The. *RIDE: The Story of Cycling in New Zealand*. Wellington: The Kennett Brothers, 2004.

Lazell, Marguerite. *Tour de France: A Hundred Years of the World's Greatest Cycle Race*. London: Carlton Books, 2003.

Maertens, Freddy, as told to Manu Adriaens, translated by Steve Hawkins. *Fall from Grace*. Hull: Ronde Publications, 1993.

Monthéour, Erwann. *Secret Défonce: Ma Vérité sur le Dopage*. Paris: J. C. Lattes, 1999.

Rasmussen, Nicolas. *On Speed: The Many Lives of Amphetamine*. New York University, 2008.

Schouten, Hank. *Tasman's Legacy: The New Zealand–Dutch Connection*. Wellington: The Netherlands Foundation, 1992.

Smeets, Mart. *Rugnummers en Ingevette Benen*. Utrecht, Netherlands: L. J. Veen, 1990.

Woodland, Les. *The Crooked Path to Victory*. San Francisco: Cycle Publishing, 2003.

Magazines and journals

Gamble, William A. 'Cycling's Flying Dutchman', *Sports Digest*, New Zealand, August 1966.

'Examiner Tour', *Road and Track Cyclist*, Australia, October 1967.

'Tabak: Gift from Holland', *Sports Digest*, New Zealand, December 1967.

Cairns, Ray. 'Tabak Better Than Ever', *N. Z. Cycling: The National Cycling Magazine of New Zealand*, July 1970.

'Hoban Gets His Classic' and 'Dutch win for Tabak'. *Cycling Weekly*, United Kingdom, April 1974.

'Somewhere between a star and a domestique', *Cycling*, United Kingdom, 27 April 1974.

Yaxley, Clayton. 'Profile – Tino Tabak', *Cycling New Zealand*, No. 25, September 1995.

Palenski, Ron. 'New Zealanders in the Tour de France', *Cycling New Zealand*, 2001.

Lucia, Alejandro, Conrad Earnest and Carlos Arribas. 'The Tour de France: A Physiological Review', *Scandinavian Journal of Medicine & Science in Sports*, 2003.

Newspaper articles

'Mann Wins Cycling, But Tabak Hero', *The Christchurch Star Sports*, 20 November 1965.
'Tabak Takes 100-mile Cycle Title', *The Christchurch Star Sports*, 4 December 1965.
'Tabak Achieves Historic Triple', *The Press* (Christchurch), 14 November 1966.
'Tabak Within Reach of Grand Slam', *The Press* (Christchurch), 10 November 1966.
'Tabak Penalty "Bit Hard to Swallow"', NZPA, 1967.
Pete Smith. 'Tremendous Tino's Second Grand Slam', unidentified article from 1967.
'More Money for NZ Cycling', *The Evening Standard* (Palmerston North), 16 January 1973.
Palenski, Ron. 'Legend back with agenda', *The Dominion* (Wellington), 21 January 1995.

Unidentified newspaper articles

'Games Choice Tabak Not Yet Naturalised', 17 May 1966.
'Tabak Dominant in 100-Mile Race', 1966.
'Tino is a New Zealander at last', 1966.
'Tabak Gets Offer to Turn Pro', 1967.
'Tabak Victimised', 1967.
'Tabak Wins Southland Cycle Tour With Thrilling Finish', 1967.
'Trouble Rides Tandem with Tino Tabak', 1967.
'Tabak in Full Cry', 1973.
'Tabak to Appear in P. N.', 1973.

Personal communication and interviews

Tino Tabak interviewed by Jonathan Kennett at his home, 2002 (tapes in New Zealand National Library), 2004, 2006, 2007, 2008, 2009.
Tino Tabak interviewed by Jonathan Kennett several times on the phone in 2009.
Colin Hollows interviewed by Jonathan Kennett in 2008.
Max Vertongen interviewed by Ian Gray in 2009.
Graeme Milner, Roger Fowler, Ross Bush and Alan Messenger interviewed by Jonathan Kennett in 2009.
Email communications in 2009 with: Les Woodland, Graeme Sycamore, Ron Palenski.

Websites

www.cyclingwebsite.net
http://en.wikipedia.org/wiki/Mont_Kemmel – Kemmelberg
www.cyclebase.nl – Tour of Twente results
www.vueltaandalucia.com
http://memoire-du-cyclisme.net/eta_tdf/presentation_tdf.php

OUT TAKES

One day, long after Tino had finished cycling, he took his car into a garage to be fixed. The mechanic recognised him and marvelled that he had ridden the Tour de France. Tino replied: 'But you can pull that whole engine to bits and put it back together again without any parts left over. I think that's amazing.'

Having tried to reconstruct Tino's cycling life, I find there are many parts that seem left over. I group them here for the reader to place them in their own way.

In the Netherlands, Gerben Tabak worked in a flour mill, and Hendrika Tabak (née Brand) was the daughter of a barber.

Gerben died of cancer in the mid-1990s. Hendrika and Corrie still live in Christchurch.

For Tino, training involved the psychology of constantly improving. He would break a training ride up into four sections and time each section. His aim was then to improve his time on at least one of the sections every time he repeated the ride. This unusual training method becomes quite challenging as the season progresses.

'He was a cheeky bastard and abused the officials something terrible.' – Colin Hollows

After the Second World War amphetamines became an established part of European cycling heritage. Fausto Coppi said in an interview aired in 1998: 'I only ever use drugs when I absolutely have to.' The interviewer asked how often that was, and Coppi replied, 'Almost always.' Manager Marcel Bidot estimated that in the 1960 Tour de France 75 per cent of the entrants used amphetamine.

In the 1970 world championships, Tino and his teammates were taken to a tent just before the event and each given an injection. They were not told what it was, but Tino, from experience, knew that it was not amphetamine.

Amphetamine was regulated from 1970, and this created a huge black market.

On his first Tour de France, in 1971, Tabak was beginning to discover that, as Hugh Dauncey and Geoff Hare put it in 2003, the Tour de France was 'a commercially oriented media creation'. In *The Tour de France, 1903–2003: A Century of Sporting Structures, Meanings and Values*, Dauncey and Hare describe the event as a 'gladiatorial contest' designed for 'the creation of heroes'.

With the introduction of television, the Tour was shortened so that the riders' speed would increase (Karl Kane, 2007), thus making it more impressive for viewers.

Flandria were the second to top team behind Molteni. They had 30 riders but only two or three were making good money. The rest were just above the minimum wage. We raced for the sport; at least to start with.

On the 1972 Tour, Tino often capitalised on the confusion created by the similarity of the French and Dutch champions' jerseys (blue, white and red, versus red, white and blue). On the steep climbs Tino whispered to the crowds, '*Poussez, poussez*' and often a patriotic but misguided Frenchman would provide an obliging push.

It's not hard to become a good sportsman, but it's hard to stay a good sportsman.

I got in a situation I thought I was Jesus Christ. I was hammered on the cross, yes, but no way was I ever that important.

Freddy Maertens claimed in his autobiography, *Fall From Grace*, that Merckx offered 100,000 francs to him and to anyone who would help him win the 1973 world championships. Maertens refused and told reporters, 'I simply will not ride for Merckx.' That upset Merckx's fans so much that, according to Maertens, they threw cold water over his legs six times during the race.

Dutch newspaper: 'Tino Tabak is a great rider in terms of strength and endurance, but he never achieved what he could have because of his stubbornness in not being willing to get involved in strategic team riding instead of streaking off by himself and then running out of steam.'

One time the people taking sample jars to the lab got robbed, at other times riders put bottles with other people's pee in it under their armpit with a little tube going down their pants and under their bum. These things go on because there is big money at stake.

Tino Tabak with Monica Valvik, whom he trained to the 1994 women's world road title in Italy. He was a tough trainer, but she was equally tough.   *Ron Palenski*

Mieke knew the dangers and all the goings on but never interfered. She supported me in my cycling 200 per cent, right up to the last day.

No one made me take anything. Why did I do it? I had to prove myself – for you! I did it to meet your expectations and to handle the pressure.

That damn ambition overrode the reality I was living.

When Tino returned to Christchurch he was cycling fit, but almost 50 years old. He was invited on a ride with Brian Fowler, Ross Bush and other top riders. They half-wheeled him, then at a particular point sprinted away, then soon after stopped at a cafe. Tino just kept on riding and did not join them for any more rides.

In 1995, the women's world road champion Monica Valvik visited New Zealand and was trained again by Tino. It is said that he drove behind her in a van at 35kmh, and if her speed dropped below that would blast the horn to make her speed up again.

The simple pleasures in life make me happier now than my greatest victory.

Tino Tabak, 2009

This street in Palmerston North was named after Tino Tabak in 1967. It is the only instance of a famous cyclist being recognised in such a way. The street developer, Monty Hollows, came from a keen cycling family and greatly admired the young Tabak. *Owen Mills*

ACKNOWLEDGEMENTS

It is surprising how many people are involved in producing one small book. Without the following people, this biography of Tino Tabak may never have been written.

First thanks must go to Tino Tabak. Since 2002 he has given several long interviews that have opened a door into the world of professional cycling that would otherwise have remained closed. Tino also granted access to his collection of photos and newspaper articles. The result speaks for itself.

The Whitireia Publishing team of Alex Pointon and Bianca Kofoed edited, typeset and managed the production of this book, under the supervision of Rachel Lawson. Elaine Hall compiled the index.

Various drafts were reviewed and edited by a generous team of experts. Many thanks to Bronwen Wall (editor and cyclist), Jim Robinson (copywriter and cyclist), Ian Gray (cycling historian and archivist), Mary MacPherson (writer), Simon Kennett (cycle writer, racer, organiser), Ron Palenski (writer, sports historian and chief executive of the Sports Hall of Fame), Ron McGann (cyclist) and Andrew McLellan (cyclist).

Recollections of life in the Netherlands during and after the Second World War, and the experiences of emigration to New Zealand, were supplied by Jeane Zee. Both Jeane and her daughter Anja Wall helped to translate Dutch newspaper articles.

Alan Messenger was interviewed and peer-reviewed the chapter on New Zealand racing. Adrian Thornton (cycling historian) supplied various interesting photos and newspaper articles. Bob Knight, cycling enthusiast and cycle collector, supplied information on the Raleigh Cycling Team.

Marleen Oud obtained photos from the Netherlands National Library.

Roger Fowler and Ross Bush provided recollections of racing in the 1960s, as did North Islanders Colin Hollows and Max Vertongen. Owen Mills provided the photo of Tabak Crescent. Selwyn Andrews made his Tabak archive available. Paul Wylie offered his recollections of the Coca-Cola tour. Dr Nick Wilson assisted with medical information. Paul Kennett and Bronwen Wall provided the diagram of the *waaier*.

Les Woodland, author of *The Unknown Tour de France* and many other books on European cycling, provided much useful information and peer-reviewed the Tour de France chapter of this book.

THE AUTHOR

Jonathan Kennett first met Tino Tabak at his country cottage in the spring of 2002. After a full-day interview, just as the tape deck was being packed away, Tino asked Jonathan to write his biography. Since then, the author has interviewed Mr Tabak several times.

Jonathan Kennett started writing in 1991 and has co-written several books including the critically acclaimed history *RIDE: the Story of Cycling in New Zealand*. He started the *Cycling Legends* series and the best-selling *Classic New Zealand Mountain Bike Rides*. He is a keen cyclist, guitarist and mountaineer.

INDEX
'TT' is the abbreviation for Tino Tabak.
Pictures in bold.

Abelshausen, Jos 55
Acht van Chaam criterium 92–93,
  106–109, **108–109**
Air New Zealand Cycling Grand Prix,
  1967 43
air resistance: role in cycling 28
amateur code for cycling 38, 42, 95–96
amateur Dutch racing career: TT's
  success 64, 66–67
Amstel Gold Race 106
Anquetil, Jacques 19, 28, 103
Arendsen, Mieke. *see* Tabak, Mieke
Armstrong, Lance 113
Australian cycle race: entered by TT 43

Baker, Alf 43, 47
Beeston, Bryce 43
Belgian Drug Brigade 120
bicycles
  bitser 18
  Carlton **22**, 23
  Flandria 70
  Holdsworth 18
  RIH 52
Black Tulip amateur cycling team 39
Blazely, Rex 43, 46–47
Bordeaux–Paris race 127–128
Broome, Jack 43
Brown, Derek 43, 46
Brown, Keith 38
Bush, Ross 42, 140
Byers, Laurie 30

Cairns, Ray 48
Canterbury Sportsman of the Year, 1966
  30, 100
Cardwell, Mr 46
Champion, Tom 13
Christchurch to Akaroa race 18, 19

Circuit of Kemzeke race 106
Circuit of Waasland race 106
Cleary, John 20, **21**, 23, 140
cobblestones: cycling on 54–55, 101,
  107, 114–115
Coca-Cola: sponsor of Tabak tour 96
combines 58, 60, 106
Commonwealth Games, Jamaica 29–30
cultural identity 13, 14, 51–52, 56
Cyclist of the Year, 1966: 30

Dalton, Warwick 29, 47
Davis, Merv 43
Dawe, Laurie 23
Dean, John **56**, 61, 96
Demeyer, Marc 117, 129
Dernys motorised bicycles **128**,
  127–128
drugs. *see* performance-enhancing
  drugs
drug testing
  for amphetamines 61–62, 150
  in prize-riding 120
  riders tainted by 103
Dulux Six Day Cycle Race
  history and description 34, **35**
  TT winner in 1966 and 1967 32, 34
Dutch Cycling Federation 62
Dutch National Road Champion,
  1972 84
Dutch professional road cycling
  championships, 1972 80–84
Dutch season of racing 69

echelon system (*waaier*) 53
Egmond aan Zee: TT's home after
  marriage 64
Examiner Tour of the North, Tasmania:
  43, 46–47

Flandria bike 70
Flandria-Velda team 117
Fowler, Roger 42, 140

Ganderton, Alf 32
Ghent–Ieper race 54–55
Ghent–Wevelgem classic 110
Gimondi, Felice 92
Goudsmit-Hoff team 77, **78–79**
   disbanding of 93
   in Dutch professional road cycling championships 80–81
   in Tour de France, 1972 84, 86–92
   TT as leader 77
Grand Prix de Menton 96–97
Grand Prix d'Orchies classic 101
Grandstand: TT featured on 25
Grave, Dave **31**, 38

Haile, Jan 130
handicap racing 18
'helping' versus 'winning' contracts: in professional racing 70–72
Hill, Graham 42
Hoban, Barry 110
Holdsworth bike 18
Hordijk, Bas 129
Hornby Wheelman cycling club 18
hour record: broken by TT in 1967 37, 48

Ineson, Tony 28, 30, **31**, 32

Janssen, Jan 81
Jenkins, Roy **41**

Kemmelberg (cobblestone section) 54
Kendell, Bill **26–27**
Kent, Harry 32
Ketting team 66
King, Gary **41**
Koning, Matthijs de **82–83**, 84
Kuiper, Hennie 66–67, 115, 140
Kuiper, Johnny 51

Lanterne Rouge (The Red Lantern) 117–118
Laurie Dawe Cycles 20
Leman, Erik 70
Litolff, Harry 38
Litolff, Mike **21**
Long, Bill 47
Lyster, Neil 96

Maertens, Freddy 93, 103, 112, 117–118, 140, 151
Mairehau Novice Cycling Club 20
Manning, Brian **31**
Manning, Kevin 34
Mars-Flandria professional team 67, 70
McDermott, Peter 46
McGregor, George 48
Menthéour, Erwann 106
Merckx, Eddy 'the Cannibal' 70, 71, 73, **74–75**, 92, 97, 103, 110, **111**, 112, 113, 119, 139, 140, 151
Messenger, Alan 25, 29
Molteni team 86, 97
Monseré, Jean-Pierre **71**

New Zealand Road Championships, 1965 29–30, **31**, 39–40
New Zealand Amateur Cycling Association
   censure of TT 32
   offered to trial TT for Olympics 58
   role in Tabak tour 95–96
New Zealand seasons and grades 19

Ocaña, Luis 73, **74–75**, 96–98, 129, 140
Oliver, Robert 96
Olympia Club 58
Olympics Games, 1968: TT's selection for 58
Onderneming, De, team 127
Opperman, Hubert 43

Papanui Primary School 14
Paris–Roubaix race 114–115

INDEX

Pellenaars, Kees 'De Pell' 78, 80–81, 84, 86, **87**, 90
Pennington, Alvyn 34
performance-enhancing drugs
 amphetamines 60–62, 121–122
 painkillers and stimulants 101–103
 in prize-riding 119–121
 steroids 120–121
 vitamin B12 32
Pollentier, Michel 117
Post, Peter **72**, 105–106, 110, 112, 140
Poulidor, Raymond 92, 97
Powell, Mal **41**
Prinsen, Wim 129
prize-riding 118–120
prizes for amateurs 39
professional team training 69
professional team: TT first offered place on 66
psychological boosting: with placebos 62, 64

race-fixing deals between riders 80–81, 84, 93, 97, 106–107, 112
race results, all events 141–145
Raleigh Team 105–106, 110, 112
Raymond, Christian 71, 113
Riccarton High School 18
RIH bike factory 52
Robinson, Neil **31**, 42
Round the Gorges Classic, 1965 **26–27**, 28–29

Schotte, Briek 71
Shirley Lodge Race 48
Simpson, Tommy 61, 139
Smith, Peter 37, 49
soigneurs 86–88, 130
Sonolor team **97**, 97–100
Sowry, Rob 46
sponsorship: for amateur cyclists 39
Springel, Herman van 71
Sword, Graeme **21**

Tabak, Corrie 15, **36**, 150
Tabak, Gerben 13–14, 16, 19, 38–39, 42, 95, 150
Tabak, Hendrika 14, 15, **15–16**, **36**, 150
Tabak, Melanie 100, 127
Tabak, Mieke 64, 78–79, **85**, 96, 100, 110, 120, 126, 127, 134–135, 152
Tabak, Paul 79, 127
Tabak, Tino
 achievements in 1966 30
 achievements in 1972 93
 achievements in 1974 106
 alcohol use 23, 32, 110, 112, 126
 childhood and education 14, **15**, 16, 18
 contempt of officialdom 37–38, 150
 crashes 131
 departure from New Zealand racing 49, 51
 disqualified in 1976 Tour de France 118
 Dutch nationality taken up 58–60
 employment: Addington Railway Workshops 18, 23; contract jobs 23; post-cycling 133–135
 favourite training ride 45
 first professional team contract 66
 impact of professional racing on 129–130
 impact of supporters 123
 initial training and racing in Amsterdam 52–53
 injuries: broken arm 58; from crash 98–100
 leadership of a team 77, 80, 88
 marriage to Mieke Arendsen 64
 military training 16, 64
 move to Rotterdam 127
 New Zealand tour 95–96
 positive test for amphetamines 62
 as a prize rider 118–120
 professional deal offered 47
 as a racing celebrity 25

Tabak, Tino (*continued*)
  racing style/tactics 18, 19, 64, 77;
    inconsistency on climbs 90; lack of
    sprint finish 28, 30
  return to New Zealand 135
  rivals and supporters 42
  success as junior in 1956 25–26, 30
  training Monica Valvik 135, 151
  White House hotel ownership 110,
    112, 126
Tabak family
  homes: Enschede 10, 51; Hornby
    15; Mt Thomas 14; Styx 13
  migration to New Zealand 9–11, 13
teams: of amateur cyclists 39
Telesport Trophy 106
Thévenet, Bernard 90
Thompson, Des 30
Thompson, Richie 30
Thorpe, Wayne 23
Timaru to Christchurch 28
time trials: TT exceptional at 26, 29
Tour de France, 1971: 70–73, **74–75**
Tour de France, 1972: 84, 86–92, **89**
Tour de France, 1973: 97–100
Tour de France, 1976: 117–118
Tour de France, New Zealanders 146
Tour of Belgium 97, 106, 112
Tour of Holland, 1978: 130–131
Tour of Levant 92
Tour of Manawatu 32
Tour of North Holland, 1970 64, 66–67

Tour of South Holland 105–106
Tour of Southland 23, 29, 32, 37
Tour of Southland, 1965 29
Tour of Twente 56, **57**

Valvik, Monica 135, **151**
Vertongen family 42
Vertongen, Max 42
Vianen, Gerard 92
village races 118–120
Vlaeminck, Erik de 70, 129
Vlaeminck, Roger de 70–71, **74–75**

waaier (echelon system) 53
Wagtmans, Marinus 'Rini' 52, 80–81,
  82–83, **87**, 90 ,**91**, 92, 140
Watson, Harry 70
wheel-sucking tactic 28, 55
White House hotel 110, 112, 126
Williams, Stan 20, 38
Windmill team 52
World Cycling Championships, 1969
  62, 63
World Cycling Championships, 1970
  66

Yaxley, Clayton 30, 38

Zijlaard, Joop 127, 128
Zoetemelk, Joop **74–75**, 80 , 84, 97,
  103, 106–107, **108–109**, 140
Zoppa-Zeus team 129–130

PREVIOUS CYCLING LEGENDS

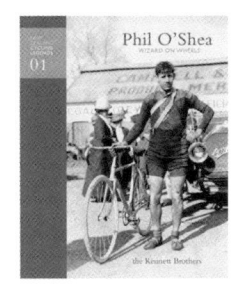

Phil O'Shea: Wizard on Wheels

Phil O'Shea is the first in a series of ten books on New Zealand's most famous cycling legends. It details the remarkable feats of a sporting superstar, whose exceptional ability attracted thousands of spectators to race appearances throughout the country. Phil O'Shea's victories, from quarter-mile sprints to 265-kilometre road races, earned this champion of champions the moniker of 'New Zealand's Greatest Cyclist'.

Harry Watson: The Mile Eater

In 1928 Harry Watson became the first New Zealander to race the Tour de France. His performances in Europe and Australia made him the most accomplished Kiwi road rider of his era. It was a time when riders were pushed to the limit, racing single-speed, fixed-wheel bikes over hundreds of kilometres per day, on rough roads of dirt and gravel. In New Zealand he won almost every long distance race he entered, and in France he finished 28th in the great Tour, which was then 5,375 kilometres long.

Bill Pratney: Never Say Die

Bill Pratney's extraordinary career had barely begun when he was involved in a terrible accident. One rider was killed, and Pratney was left for dead on the side of the road. Against the odds this iron man recovered. He not only took up racing again, but was soon winning New Zealand championship titles on track and road.

Warwick Dalton: The Lone Eagle

After dominating on track and road in New Zealand, Dalton crossed the globe and achieved remarkable results as an amateur in Europe. He then moved to Australia and switched to the professional ranks, where he was a popular success, especially on the lucrative six-day track circuit.

For more books on New Zealand cycling go to www.kennett.co.nz